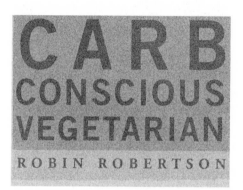

# CARB
## CONSCIOUS
## VEGETARIAN

### ROBIN ROBERTSON

RODALE

LIVE YOUR WHOLE LIFE™

Every day our brands
connect with and inspire
millions of people to live
a life of the mind, body,
spirit — a whole life.

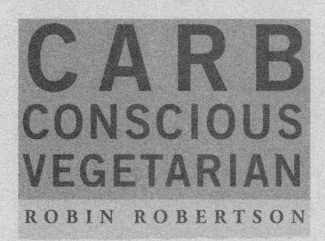

# CARB CONSCIOUS VEGETARIAN

### ROBIN ROBERTSON

## 150 DELICIOUS RECIPES

## FOR A

## HEALTHY LIFESTYLE

RODALE

Printed in the United States of America
Rodale Inc. makes every effort to use acid-free ∞, recycled paper ♻.

Book design by Christopher Rhoads

Illustrations by Paul Woods

**Library of Congress Cataloging-in-Publication Data**

Robertson, Robin (Robin G.)

    Carb-conscious vegetarian : 150 delicious recipes for a healthy lifestyle / Robin Robertson.

        p.     cm.

    Includes index.

    ISBN-13 978–1–59486–123–9 paperback

    ISBN-10 1–59486–123–4 paperback

    1. Vegetarian cookery.    2. Low-carbohydrate diet—Recipes.    I. Title.

TX837.R62374   2005

   641.5'636—dc22                         2005008167

**Distributed to the trade by Holtzbrinck Publishers**

2   4   6   8   10   9   7   5   3   1   paperback

**RODALE**
LIVE YOUR WHOLE LIFE™

We inspire and enable people to improve their lives and the world around them
For more of our products visit **rodalestore.com** or call 800-848-4735

To my sister, Carole

# CONTENTS

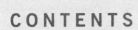

# ACKNOWLEDGMENTS

Many helpful people played a role in making this book a reality. My deepest appreciation goes to Laura Frisk, Christina O'Brien, Gina Myers, Gloria Siegel, Steve Young, and Hanna and Philip Schein for testing recipes with great skill and enthusiasm. To my husband, Jon Robertson, many thanks for pitching in whenever there was a need, be it tasting and testing recipes or keeping my computer files organized. Much gratitude goes to my dear friends Jannette Patterson, Carol and Francis Janes, and Simone Gabbay, R.N.C.P., for their help and support. Special thanks to Brenda Davis, R.D., for her expert advice and guidance. I also wish to acknowledge Neal Barnard, M.D.; Joel Fuhrman, M.D.; and Michael Klaper, M.D., whose groundbreaking books on vegan diet and nutrition have long been an inspiration to me. Many thanks to my agent, Stacey Glick of Dystel & Goderich Literary Management, for her ongoing support and encouragement. I also wish to thank my editor, Pamela Adler, for her insights and expertise, as well as Miriam Backes, Margot Schupf, and everyone at Rodale who was involved in the project.

# INTRODUCTION

After going vegetarian in 1987, I was often asked, "Are you getting enough protein?" I always answered in the affirmative, since my diet included an abundance of protein-rich beans, legumes, and soy products. But years (and extra pounds) later, I realized that, while I was carefully monitoring my protein intake, I had paid scarce attention to carbohydrates. Despite the fact that many of the carbs I ate were "good" carbs such as brown rice and other whole grains, I also ate more than my share of refined carbs in the forms of white bread, white pasta, white rice, and white sugar. I was no stranger to starchy vegetables such as potatoes or corn either.

Some people, vegetarians and otherwise, may be able to load up on carbs without negative results. However, others gain weight. I'm not blaming the vegetarian diet for this, rather the uninformed choices people make when choosing a plant-based diet.

In my own case, I naively thought that since I was eating no food containing cholesterol or saturated fat, I could eat virtually anything. Boy, was I wrong. I eventually realized that the tasty mountain of ziti on my plate wasn't going to help me lose weight. I figured out that those mega-bagels weren't the ideal choice either. Still, the more refined carbs I ate, the more I wanted.

Once I turned 50, I resolved to do something about my sidetracked diet. Go back to eating meat? Never. As an ethical vegan, my love and respect for animals are more important to me than my dress size. Besides, I knew it wasn't the vegetables and tofu that packed on the extra pounds. After much research, I discovered that the one answer to losing weight could be found in eliminating refined carbohydrates. It seems that while many people can thrive on a well-balanced vegetarian diet that may include refined carbs, others need to monitor their carbohydrate intake more carefully in order to keep their weight down.

I knew I wasn't alone in my struggle with refined carbohydrates. For several years now, other vegetarians, frustrated by the ubiquity of the meat-oriented low-carb diet craze, have been asking me for low-carb recipes with the vegetarian in mind. It is in response to them that I've written this book.

I'm proud to present these 150 nutrient-rich vegetarian recipes. They contain no refined carbohydrates, such as white bread, white rice, sugar, or pasta. Instead, the recipes focus on nutrient-rich plant-based foods, such as soy in all its forms, including tofu and tempeh, and a wide variety of vegetables, beans, legumes, whole grains, fruits, nuts, and seeds. I've compiled recipes that provide the best of both worlds—the benefits of a vegetarian diet that is also relatively low in carbohydrates. And because enjoyment of food is tantamount to our well-being, these full-flavored recipes are designed for dining pleasure in addition to good health.

# CARB
## CONSCIOUS
## VEGETARIAN

### ROBIN ROBERTSON

# CHAPTER ONE

# A FIRM FOUNDATION

During the "low-carb" craze of the early 2000s, much of the hype emphasized consuming large amounts of meat and cheese and avoiding carbohydrates. This flew in the face of a healthy vegetarian diet, since plant-based ingredients contain carbohydrates. The fact is, commonsense dietary guidelines on carbohydrate consumption are important for good health and weight control, whether you eat meat or not.

Vegetarians, and others who avoid animal products, can be healthy and stay trim through an enlightened understanding and use of "good" carbohydrates, while eliminating "bad" carbohydrates and still eating satisfying meals. This cookbook shows the delicious and sensible way to win the carbohydrate game and proves that "carb-conscious" vegetarian recipes are a practical and preferable alternative to "low-carb."

The secret is to break free from the trap of relying on white bread, pasta, potatoes, and rice at mealtime. The recipes in this book eliminate refined carbohydrates, so you can cut back on carbs without sacrificing necessary fiber, phytochemicals, and other important nutrients. Because the recipes are vegetarian, they also leave out the saturated fat and cholesterol usually associated with low-carb diets.

I considered all of these factors when deciding what ingredients to feature in a "carb-conscious" vegetarian cookbook. This is a "moderately low-carb/all-good-carb" vegetarian cookbook. Thanks to the work done by pioneering medical doctors such as Dean Ornish, John McDougall, Neal Barnard, Joel Fuhrman, and others, certain flaws of trendy high-protein, very low-carbohydrate diets that emphasize meat, eggs, and cheese are becoming better understood. These experts explain that people don't need animal products to lose weight or to stay healthy. Many vegetables are more than 30 percent protein and provide the body with high energy and stamina without relying on the artery-clogging animal products that have been linked to cardiovascular disease and cancer. The recipes in this book provide you with all the benefits of a healthy plant-based diet.

# The Vegetarian Call for Low-Carb

Writing vegetarian cookbooks often brings me into contact with people seeking recipes and cooking advice. The most frequent request I receive is for low-carb vegetarian recipes. Obviously, there's a need for a collection of recipes that answers the call of carb-conscious vegetarians who want to know how to cook delicious meals containing more moderate proportions of carbohydrates.

*Carb-Conscious Vegetarian* provides mouthwatering recipes for meat- and dairy-free meals that scale back the carbohydrates, primarily by eliminating refined carbs, while delivering nutrient-rich protein, fiber, vitamins, and minerals—good news for people who want creative and flavorful recipes for vitality and good health. As a former chef, my goal wasn't to write a diet book but a healthy lifestyle cookbook with delicious recipes that are adaptable enough to please anyone in your household.

## COMMON SENSE

Regardless of whether or not you're on a "diet," there are some commonsense denominators for a healthy lifestyle. A regular exercise routine plus wise food choices in moderate portions are important factors in weight control and good health.

# Importance of Natural Whole Foods in the Diet

For optimum health, it is best for everyone, whether vegetarian or nonvegetarian, to avoid refined carbohydrates. No matter whether you are maintaining your weight or you want to lose a few pounds, you still need to use moderation when eating foods that are higher in healthy, good-for-you carbohydrates, such as whole grains, beans, and root vegetables. (See Appendix A, "Carbohydrate Content of Common Foods," on page 213.) There are many benefits to a well-balanced plant-based diet consisting of dark leafy greens and other vegetables, whole grains, beans, nuts, seeds, and fruits. When you sit down to dinner, the best rule of thumb is to eat larger portions of green vegetables and other lower-carb foods and a moderate portion of the healthy higher-carb foods.

The recipes in *Carb-Conscious Vegetarian* are for anyone, whether you're trying to lose weight or you just want to eat a healthy plant-based diet. In addition, these recipes provide added health benefits since most are high in fiber and completely cholesterol free. They use no animal products, including cheese or other dairy products that are very high in saturated fat and cholesterol. However, for those wishing to include some dairy foods in their diet, certain recipes are followed by a dairy option that may be substituted for a dairy-free ingredient. Be aware, however, that if you choose to use dairy, you will be adding fat and cholesterol to the recipe.

The recipes in this book make use of a wide variety of vegetables, ranging from asparagus to zucchini, using moderate amounts of protein-rich beans, whole grains, nuts, and seeds. High-starch vegetables such as potatoes and corn are avoided, and higher-glycemic vegetables are used in moderation (see "Carbology 101" on page 7). Commercial vegetarian meat alternative products are included, as well as soy products such as tofu, tempeh, and edamame. Flavors are enhanced with a variety of herbs, spices, condiments, and cooking methods.

The tempting desserts emphasize all-natural ingredients such as fresh fruit, protein-rich nuts, heart-healthy soy, and the natural sweeteners agave syrup and stevia (artificial sweeteners are not used). Cocoa, extracts, and a limited use of whole grain flours also help to produce sweet treats that provide good nutrition with great taste and no empty calories.

# Ingredients Used in the Book

As I developed the recipes for this book, I focused as much as possible on using natural whole food ingredients for maximum nutrition, combined with herbs, spices, and other seasonings for maximum flavor. The recipes are designed to be flexible for you and your family, whether you are on a weight loss plan or simply wanting to eat healthy. They dovetail nicely into the various phases of many of the low-carb diets, although this book is not a diet book itself.

## Oils

For sautéing or stir-frying, recipes usually call for 1 tablespoon of olive oil or, in some cases, canola or another vegetable oil. If you wish to reduce the amount of oil further, you can use a nonstick skillet with half the amount of oil (in most cases) and still produce successful recipes. Or reduce the oil even further by substituting a cooking spray for the oil. In addition, a cooking spray may be used instead of oil for oiling pans and baking dishes.

## Sweeteners

Deciding what sweeteners to use in this book presented a particular challenge. Of course, refined sugar is out. At the same time, I don't recommend using artificial sweeteners. It's not necessary to completely eliminate all sweeteners—for example, organic blackstrap molasses is loaded with calcium and iron. You don't need to use much, and it can significantly improve the overall nutritional value of the diet.

My personal choices for everyday use are two diverse yet natural sweeteners: stevia and agave syrup.

Stevia is an herb indigenous to South America. It is widely used as a sweetener in South America and Asia and is gaining popularity in North America, where a number of different companies are producing it. Stevia is vastly sweeter than sugar, and the quality, flavor, and sweetness of the various brands vary widely. In addition, certain varieties have a slightly bitter aftertaste. You may want to experiment a bit to discover a brand and sweetness level you like. Stevia is available in natural food stores in both a powdered and a liquid extract form. One teaspoon of stevia is equal in sweetness to 1 cup of sugar. Stevia can be used in both cooking and baking. For more information on stevia, check out *The Stevia Cookbook* by Ray Sahelian and Donna Gates or visit www.stevia.net.

# CARBOLOGY 101

*Carbohydrates* are the starches and sugars in foods. They are a plant's way of storing the sun's energy, and they're the preferred energy source for the human body. At one point, simple carbohydrates (sugars) were thought of as "bad" and complex carbohydrates were thought of as "good," but this classification is misleading. Rather than focusing on simple and complex carbohydrates as the "bad guys" and "good guys," we need to look at the overall nutritional value of the food in question, its fiber content, and its effects on blood sugar.

• *Net carbohydrates,* a term that has come into recent use, refers to the amount of carbohydrates in a food after subtracting the carbohydrates that move through the intestine largely unabsorbed (generally, fiber, resistant starches, and sugar alcohols).

• The *glycemic index (GI)* ranks foods based on their effect on blood sugar. The GI of a food is determined by many factors, including the type and amount of fiber, the types of sugar and starch, the amount of fat, the density of the food, the size of the food particles, and the food's acidity, to name a few. Foods with a low GI release their natural sugars slowly, thus keeping blood sugar steady to stave off hunger. The GI must be used with consideration of other factors, such as the overall nutritional value of the food. A glycemic index chart is provided in Appendix B on page 223.

• The *glycemic load (GL)* is used for assessing a food's overall impact on blood sugar, which takes into account the amount of carbohydrate consumed, in addition to the GI of the food. (GL equals the amount of carbohydrate in a food multiplied by the GI.) The GL is considered a better indicator of a food's impact on blood sugar than the GI alone. Examples of foods with high and low glycemic loads are shown on page 226.

It is important to note that many healthful or "good" carbohydrates—that is, certain vegetables and fruits—have a fairly high glycemic index. These include carrots, beets, parsnips, winter squash, and sweet potatoes. Additionally, many deep-fried foods and fatty desserts have a much lower glycemic index. It doesn't take a rocket scientist (or a dietitian, for that matter) to realize that carrots and squash are better nutritionally than fried foods and fatty desserts.

We rarely eat foods in isolation. For example, we will eat a potato with a salad and some beans. All of these other foods help to moderate the glycemic effect of the potato. It makes no sense to sacrifice protective dietary components for the sake of slightly fewer grams of carbs. It is better to eat these foods in moderation, so your body can enjoy the benefits of the phytochemicals, micronutrients, and vitamins that they have to offer.

Nutritious foods such as beans, whole grains, fruits, and many vegetables contain a significant amount of carbs, but they are also rich in fiber, phytochemicals, and other nutrients necessary for good health. The secret is a low glycemic index. Additionally, if we're not loading up on the empty calories found in refined carbs, we'll feel naturally satisfied longer.

## THE CARBOHYDRATE CONUNDRUM

If you look around the world, the lowest rates of obesity and chronic diseases occur where populations consume the greatest proportion of their calories as carbohydrates. This would seem to be a contradiction, yet it is easily explained.

When carbohydrates come from whole plant foods, as they do for much of the world's population, they are consistently found to have a positive impact on good health, because they still possess their fiber, phytochemicals, vitamins, minerals, and other valuable components. In North America, carbohydrates tend to be consumed as refined, processed foods, such as white flour breads, baked goods, pretzels, crackers, soft drinks, and candy. When such foods are used as the primary sources of carbohydrates, negative health consequences result.

When carbohydrate-rich foods are refined, almost everything of value is removed before we eat them. As an example, when wheat is refined to make white flour, the most healthful parts of the plant—the germ and the bran—are removed. During this process, we throw away about 70 to 80 percent of the vitamins and minerals, 80 to 90 percent of the fiber, and 95 percent of the protective phytochemicals. We are left with the endosperm—starch. But we don't stop there—we take that starch (i.e., white flour) and add awful stuff such as hydrogenated fats, salt, sugar, preservatives, and artificial colors and flavors.

Agave syrup comes from a native plant of Mexico. It is 30 to 40 percent sweeter than sugar. While it is not especially low in carbohydrates, its advantage is its high fructose content, which means a low glycemic index. Agave juice was sometimes called "honey water" by the Aztecs, because when the leaves and root are cut, the liquid pours out. In recipes, agave syrup should be used like honey or other liquid sweeteners. Approximately ¾ cup of agave syrup can be used to replace 1 cup of sugar. Agave syrup can be used in cooking and baking and is available at natural food stores or through online mail-order sources.

## Stocking the Pantry

When stocking a healthy-carb vegetarian pantry, it's important to keep an ample supply of fresh vegetables on hand along with soy foods, whole grains, nuts, and condiments that will keep your meals interesting.

# How to Use This Book

While the benefits of a plant-based diet are numerous, there are still vegetarians who have weight control issues. The recent low-carb craze has made society "carbophobic," so it's important for vegetarians to realize that they can still follow a sensible diet that is reasonably low in carbs by mainly eliminating refined carbohydrates.

A simple way to improve one's diet is by replacing white rice, pasta, and white potatoes at mealtimes with whole grains such as brown rice, bulgur, and quinoa. Add an extra serving of vegetables at dinner. Begin your dinner with a salad or a bowl of soup. At lunchtime, consider eating hearty soups or salads instead of sandwiches. Or, if you do make sandwiches, be sure to use whole grain or sprouted breads instead of those made with refined flours. Replace empty-calorie, high-fat, or sugary snacks with nutrient-rich choices such as fresh fruit, raw vegetables and dip, or a small handful of nuts. Strive to eliminate desserts made with refined flours and sugar, opting for more healthful desserts made with fresh fruits, nuts, and natural sweeteners.

I cannot stress enough that this is a cookbook, not a diet book. However, if you're following a diet plan, whether through your doctor or via the latest bestseller, the recipes in this

## THE BIG PICTURE

If you want to moderate your carbohydrate intake and improve the nutritional quality of your diet, be sure to look at the big picture. Here are some tips.

• Choose mainly whole plant foods. Beans, whole grains, vegetables, fruits, nuts, and seeds are nutritional powerhouses.

• Minimize or avoid refined carbohydrate foods. White flour and sugar-laden products deliver a lot of calories, offer little satiety, and are nutritional washouts.

• Consider the glycemic index (GI) and the glycemic load (GL) of the foods you are eating. Within each food category, generally select those that have a lower GI and GL. At the same time, remember to consider the overall nutritional value of the food and its fiber and phytochemical content when making your choice. See the charts in Appendix B on pages 223–226.

• Beware of beverages. They can pack on the carbs, especially refined sugars. Soft drinks, gourmet coffees, fruit drinks, and many alcoholic beverages are loaded with sugar. Instead, quench your thirst with water, herbal teas, or other noncaloric beverages.

book can help you to prepare healthful vegetarian meals that should fit into most any diet plan. These recipes contain no refined carbs and are low to moderate in healthy carbs, low in fat, free of cholesterol, high in fiber, and chock-full of phytochemicals and micronutrients. Best of all, they're easy to prepare and taste great.

## DON'T BE FOOLED

Did you know that the glycemic index (GI) has little to do with providing maximum nutrition? Many high-fat, processed foods have a lower GI than many healthful, whole plant foods. For example, a plain chocolate bar has a lower GI than brown rice or carrots. Common sense has a lot to do with food choices. Brown rice or carrots may have a higher glycemic index than a candy bar or a piece of cake, but it's obvious which will be better for you. (See the Glycemic Index Chart on pages 223–226.)

# CHAPTER TWO

# VIRTUOUS APPETIZERS AND RIGHTEOUS SNACKS

The best part about the recipes in this chapter is that they seem like rich indulgences. In truth, they only taste that way. These recipes have been crafted to be enjoyed as healthful, guilt-free first-course party foods and snacks. They're low in carbs, high in fiber, and rich in vitamins, minerals, and phytonutrients. As a bonus, many of them are also reasonably low in calories as well as high in protein. All of them are free of cholesterol. So at your next party, when you don't know what to serve because you don't know who's on what diet, you can choose from any of these tasty tidbits and be confident that you will satisfy everyone in your hungry crowd.

# GUACAMAME

*Creamy, green, and delicious, this dip is lower in carbs and higher in protein than your standard guacamole. Using protein-rich edamame to replace some of the avocado makes it lower in fat, too. Edamame, or green soybeans, are available either fresh or frozen, both in and out of the pod.*

1 cup fresh or frozen shelled edamame, cooked

1 small ripe avocado, pitted and peeled

1 can (4 ounces) chopped green chiles, drained

2 teaspoons fresh lime juice

1 tablespoon finely chopped onion

1 teaspoon chopped garlic

$\frac{1}{8}$ teaspoon ground cumin

Salt and freshly ground black pepper

Assorted cut raw vegetables for dipping

In a food processor or blender, combine the edamame, avocado, chiles, and lime juice. Process until smooth. Add the onion, garlic, cumin, and salt and pepper to taste. Pulse to blend in, leaving some texture. Transfer to a serving bowl and serve with the raw vegetables.

**SERVES 4**

Per serving: 110 calories, 6 g fat, 6 g protein, 9 g carbohydrates, 4 g fiber, 0 mg cholesterol, 82 mg sodium

# CELERY STUFFED WITH SUN-DRIED TOMATO HUMMUS

*The addition of sun-dried tomatoes brightens the color and flavor of traditional chickpea and sesame dip.*

1½ cups cooked chickpeas

½ cup tahini paste

3 tablespoons fresh lemon juice

2 tablespoons sun-dried tomatoes, soaked and coarsely chopped

2 tablespoons water

2 cloves garlic

½ teaspoon salt

4–5 ribs celery, cut into 1½" pieces

In a blender or food processor, combine the chickpeas, tahini, lemon juice, tomatoes, water, garlic, and salt. Blend until smooth. Taste to adjust the seasoning. Use a knife to spread the mixture into the hollow part of the celery pieces and arrange on a platter.

**SERVES 6**

Per serving: 198 calories, 12 g fat, 8 g protein, 18 g carbohydrates, 4 g fiber, 0 mg cholesterol, 485 mg sodium

# WHITE BEAN HUMMUS WITH GREEN CHILES AND BLACK OLIVES

*Made with white beans instead of chickpeas, this unusual hummus has more surprises in store with the tantalizing inclusion of green chiles and kalamata olives.*

1½ cups cooked white beans

½ cup tahini paste

2 cloves garlic

3 tablespoons fresh lemon juice

¼ cup chopped canned green chiles

¼ cup chopped kalamata olives

Salt and freshly ground black pepper

In a blender or food processor, combine the beans, tahini, garlic, lemon juice, chiles, olives, and salt and pepper to taste. Blend until smooth. Taste to adjust the seasoning. Transfer to a bowl, cover, and refrigerate for at least 1 hour before serving to allow flavors time to develop.

**SERVES 6**

Per serving: 194 calories, 11 g fat, 8 g protein, 18 g carbohydrates, 4 g fiber, 0 mg cholesterol, 69 mg sodium

## SNACK ATTACKS

Consider these ideas for smart snacking:

• A small bowl of cherries, blueberries, or strawberries

• A ripe peach or plum

• Raw vegetables with hummus, peanut butter, or almond butter

• A small handful of pistachio nuts

• Apple slices spread with almond butter

• A small handful of roasted soy nuts

• Cooked and cooled edamame in the pod

• A nutritious smoothie made with soy and berries

# JALAPEÑO HUMMUS WITH JICAMA DIPPERS

*The spicy bite of jalapeño in a creamy hummus contrasts with the cooling crunch of jicama. A native of Mexico, jicama is a root vegetable resembling a potato that can be eaten raw or cooked. Best of all, it's reasonably low in carbs and rich in potassium and vitamin C. Peel the jicama just before using, as it can discolor when left out too long.*

- 1 clove garlic
- 1½ cups cooked chickpeas
- 2–3 tablespoons chopped jalapeño chile peppers (canned or jarred, but not pickled)
- ¼ cup tahini paste
- 2 tablespoons fresh lemon juice
- ½ teaspoon salt
- 2–3 tablespoons water
- 1–2 jicamas

Place the garlic in a food processor and process until chopped. Add the chickpeas and jalapeños and process until combined. Add the tahini, lemon juice, salt, and 2 tablespoons of the water. Process until smooth, adding the remaining 1 tablespoon water if necessary for a creamy texture. Transfer to a small bowl.

When ready to serve, peel the jicamas and cut in half lengthwise. With the cut side down, slice the jicama halves lengthwise into ¼" strips and arrange on a platter with the bowl of the hummus.

**SERVES 6**

Per serving: 154 calories, 6 g fat, 7 g protein, 21 g carbohydrates, 8 g fiber, 0 mg cholesterol, 419 mg sodium

# SNOW PEAS STUFFED WITH CILANTRO HUMMUS

*If you love cilantro, this fresh, light, and lovely "green-on-green" appetizer will be a hit. Letting the hummus stand for an hour or so in the fridge before serving will allow the flavor of the cilantro to intensify.*

36 snow peas

1 clove garlic, crushed

1½ cups cooked chickpeas

¼ cup tahini paste

3 tablespoons fresh lemon juice

½ teaspoon salt

⅛ teaspoon ground red pepper

1½ cups chopped fresh cilantro

2 tablespoons water

Trim the snow peas, removing the strings. Lightly blanch the snow peas in boiling water for about 1 minute, then drain and plunge them into ice water to stop the cooking process. Drain again, then set aside and pat dry.

Process the garlic in a food processor until finely chopped, then add the chickpeas and process to break them up. Add the tahini, lemon juice, salt, ground red pepper, and cilantro and blend until well combined. With the machine running, slowly stream in the water and process until smooth. Spoon the hummus into a pastry bag fitted with a star tip.

Being careful not to tear the pea pods, pipe the hummus into the open side of the snow peas and arrange them decoratively on a serving tray.

**SERVES 6**

Per serving: 145 calories, 6 g fat, 6 g protein, 17 g carbohydrates, 5 g fiber, 0 mg cholesterol, 456 mg sodium

# SKINNY DIP WITH VEGETABLES IN THE RAW

*The familiar spinach-artichoke dip is lightened with soy and spiced up with green chiles. In addition to being low in carbs, it's low in calories and fat. Best of all, since it tastes good enough to eat with a spoon, you won't need bread or crackers, although an assortment of raw veggies is a great idea.*

*Another change from the original warm dip: You can dive right in cold—just like skinny dipping! In fact, the dip tastes better after it sits in the fridge for a while to allow the flavors to blend together and intensify, so I would suggest chilling for an hour or more, even overnight.*

1 package (10 ounces) frozen chopped spinach, thawed

1 can (14 ounces) artichoke hearts, drained, or 1 package (10 ounces) frozen artichokes, cooked

1 can (4 ounces) chopped green chiles, drained

2 tablespoons finely chopped scallions, or to taste

½ cup firm tofu, well drained and crumbled

1 tablespoon fresh lemon juice

¾ teaspoon salt

⅛ teaspoon freshly ground black pepper

Assorted raw vegetables for dipping

Cook the spinach in boiling salted water for 1 to 2 minutes. Drain well and set aside to cool. Once cool, squeeze the excess moisture from the spinach and set aside.

Chop the artichokes in a food processor. Add the chiles, scallions, tofu, lemon juice, salt, pepper, and reserved spinach. Process until well blended. Transfer to a bowl, cover, and refrigerate for at least 1 hour before serving with raw vegetables.

**SERVES 6**

Per serving: 50 calories, 1 g fat, 4 g protein, 7 g carbohydrates, 4 g fiber, 0 mg cholesterol, 409 mg sodium

**Variation:** Substitute yogurt or sour cream for the tofu.

# ROASTED EGGPLANT DIP WITH CRUNCHY THREE-SEED CRACKERS

*This recipe was inspired by the high-powered protein-dense crackers made in food dehydrators that are widely used by raw foodists. While this cracker recipe could successfully be made in a food dehydrator, I've developed it for oven use. The eggplant dip is similar to baba ghannouj.*

## CRACKERS

½ cup raw pumpkin seeds

½ cup raw sunflower seeds

¾ cup golden flaxseeds or sesame seeds

¼ teaspoon onion powder

¼ teaspoon celery salt

¼ teaspoon salt

2 tablespoons finely chopped fresh flat-leaf parsley

¼ cup water

## DIP

1 large eggplant

1 clove garlic, crushed

⅓ cup tahini paste

2 tablespoons chopped fresh flat-leaf parsley

3 tablespoons fresh lemon juice

½ teaspoon salt

¼ teaspoon ground cumin

⅛ teaspoon ground red pepper

*For the crackers:* Preheat the oven to 275°F.

In a blender or food processor, grind the pumpkin seeds, sunflower seeds, and ½ cup of the flaxseeds or sesame seeds to a powder. Add the onion powder, celery salt, salt, parsley, and water. Blend in short bursts to mix into a dough.

Line a baking sheet with parchment paper and spread the dough out flat on it. Top with another piece of parchment paper and roll the dough out evenly and thinly with a rolling pin (or use your hands to press the dough out as thinly as you can) to make approximately a 12" square. Remove the top layer of paper and sprinkle on the remaining ¼ cup flaxseeds or sesame seeds; press the seeds into the dough to embed the seeds. Use a sharp knife to score the dough into 24 crackers (about 3" × 2" each).

Bake the crackers until lightly browned, about 3 hours. For crisper crackers, turn the oven off and leave them in a while longer. Once cooled completely, the crackers may be stored at room temperature in a tightly covered container.

*For the dip:* Preheat the oven to 450°F. Place the eggplant on a baking sheet and bake, turning frequently, until the skin is blistered all over, about 30 minutes. Place the eggplant in a paper bag until cool enough to handle, 15 to 20 minutes, then peel off and discard the charred skin. Squeeze the eggplant to remove the bitter juices.

Transfer the eggplant pulp to a food processor and blend with the garlic, tahini, parsley, lemon juice, salt, cumin, and ground red pepper. Taste to adjust the seasoning. You should have about 2 cups of dip. Transfer to a bowl, then cover and refrigerate until ready to serve.

The dip tastes best served at room temperature. Place the bowl of dip in the center of a platter and surround with the crackers.

**SERVES 8**

Per serving: 256 calories, 19 g fat, 10 g protein, 15 g carbohydrates, 6 g fiber, 0 mg cholesterol, 270 mg sodium

## TEXAS TWO-STEP CAVIAR

*Eggplant dip is sometimes called "poor man's caviar," and a spread made with black-eyed peas is called "Texas caviar." Combine elements from both for a delicious protein-packed spread that can be used to stuff celery, spread on whole grain crackers, or thin as a dip for raw vegetables.*

1 eggplant, halved lengthwise

3 cloves garlic, unpeeled

1 cup cooked black-eyed peas

2 tablespoons finely chopped onion

¼ cup finely chopped fresh flat-leaf parsley

2 tablespoons olive oil

2 tablespoons red wine vinegar

½ teaspoon Dijon mustard

⅛ teaspoon ground cumin

⅛ teaspoon dried oregano

Salt and freshly ground black pepper

Preheat the oven to 400°F. Place the eggplant in a lightly oiled shallow baking dish, cut side down. Add the garlic cloves and bake until the eggplant is tender, about 30 minutes. Set aside to cool.

Peel the eggplant, squeeze out any liquid, and transfer the pulp to a food processor. Peel the garlic and add the pulp to the processor along with the black-eyed peas, onion, parsley, oil, vinegar, mustard, cumin, oregano, and salt and pepper to taste. Pulse until just mixed, retaining a coarse texture. Scrape the mixture into a bowl and taste to adjust the seasoning. Cover and refrigerate for at least a few hours to allow the flavors to blend.

**SERVES 6**

Per serving: 71 calories, 5 g fat, 1 g protein, 7 g carbohydrates, 2 g fiber, 0 mg cholesterol, 15 mg sodium

# WATERCRESS WASABI DIP WITH CRISP AND CRUNCHY CRUDITÉ PLATTER

*This zesty dip should be made within a few hours of serving time since the flavor of the wasabi becomes more pronounced the longer it sits. For the crudités, use celery sticks, cucumber spears, fennel sticks, bell pepper strips, radishes, and so forth.*

1 cup packed chopped watercress
½ cup soy mayonnaise
½ cup tofu sour cream
1½ teaspoons wasabi paste, or to taste
Salt
Assorted cut vegetables for dipping

In a food processor or blender, combine the watercress, mayonnaise, sour cream, wasabi, and salt to taste. Blend until smooth, scraping down the sides several times with a rubber spatula. Transfer the dipping sauce to a serving bowl. Place it on a serving tray surrounded by the cut vegetables.

**SERVES 4**

Per serving: 76 calories, 9 g fat, 1 g protein, 4 g carbohydrates, 0 g fiber, 0 mg cholesterol, 159 mg sodium

**Variation:** Substitute regular mayonnaise for the soy mayonnaise and dairy sour cream for the tofu sour cream.

# CUCUMBER ROUNDS TOPPED WITH BLACK OLIVE AND MUSHROOM TAPENADE

*The addition of mushrooms to the tapenade helps round out the stronger flavors of the black olives, garlic, and capers. Serving the tapenade on cucumber rounds makes this a decidedly low-carb appetizer.*

2 teaspoons extra virgin olive oil

4 ounces white mushrooms, coarsely chopped

Salt and freshly ground black pepper

3 cloves garlic

1½ cups pitted kalamata olives

1 tablespoon capers, rinsed and drained, plus additional for garnish

½ cup chopped fresh flat-leaf parsley, plus additional for garnish

2 English cucumbers, peeled decoratively and cut into ¼" rounds (see note)

Heat the oil in a large skillet over medium-high heat. Add the mushrooms, season with salt and pepper, and cook until the mushrooms release their juices, about 5 minutes. Drain well and set aside to cool.

In a food processor, chop the garlic. Add the cooled mushrooms, olives, capers, parsley, and salt and pepper to taste. Pulse to combine the ingredients. Transfer the tapenade to a bowl.

Place the cucumber rounds on paper towels to absorb some of the moisture, then spoon a small amount of tapenade onto each round and arrange on a serving tray. Garnish each round with a parsley leaf or small caper.

**SERVES 6**

Per serving: 120 calories, 10 g fat, 2 g protein, 7 g carbohydrates, 1 g fiber, 0 mg cholesterol, 587 mg sodium

Note: Use a vegetable peeler, a channel zester, or the tines of a fork to create a decorative appearance along the length of each cucumber before slicing it into rounds.

# LETTUCE-WRAPPED VEGETABLE SPRING ROLLS WITH SPICY PEANUT SAUCE

*Fresh, light, delicious—and low in carbs. What could be better? Be careful not to overstuff the rolls or they can get a tad messy, but with flavors this good, you probably won't mind.*

1½ tablespoons low-sodium tamari soy sauce

1 tablespoon fresh lime juice

¼ cup reduced-fat peanut butter

1 clove garlic, crushed

1 teaspoon finely chopped fresh ginger

¼ teaspoon crushed red-pepper flakes

4–5 tablespoons water

6 large soft leaves lettuce (Boston or leaf lettuce is a good choice)

1 cup finely shredded napa cabbage

1 small red bell pepper, thinly sliced

1 cup fresh bean sprouts, blanched

½ cup chopped fresh cilantro

In a blender or food processor, combine the tamari, lime juice, peanut butter, garlic, ginger, and crushed red-pepper flakes. Add 4 tablespoons of the water and blend until smooth, adding up to 1 tablespoon additional water if the sauce is too thick. Taste to adjust the seasoning. Transfer to a small bowl and set aside.

Place a lettuce leaf on a sheet of plastic wrap that has been laid out on a flat work surface. Arrange a small amount of the cabbage, bell pepper, bean sprouts, and cilantro on the bottom third of the leaf. Bring the bottom edge over the filling and fold in the sides tightly. Roll up gently but tightly, using the plastic wrap to help you roll it up; remove the plastic. Place the roll, seam side down, on a serving platter. Repeat with the remaining ingredients. When all the rolls have been assembled, serve them with the reserved sauce.

**SERVES 4**

Per serving: 120 calories, 8 g fat, 6 g protein, 8 g carbohydrates, 2 g fiber, 0 mg cholesterol, 426 mg sodium

## BELGIAN ENDIVE WITH ROASTED
## RED PEPPER–WALNUT SPREAD

*This elegant appetizer is easy to prepare—and very quick if you use jarred roasted peppers. The lovely contrast of the vivid red spread against the pale green leaves makes a striking display. The protein-rich walnuts are packed with vitamins, minerals, and antioxidants, including vitamin E, potassium, vitamin B6, and magnesium. Walnuts are also high in omega-3s and, according to the U.S. Food and Drug Administration, they may help reduce the risk of heart disease.*

2 red bell peppers, halved and seeded, or 1 jar (9 ounces) roasted red
   peppers, drained

½ cup walnuts

1 clove garlic, halved

2 tablespoons tomato paste

1 tablespoon olive oil

1 teaspoon finely chopped fresh thyme or ½ teaspoon dried thyme

½ teaspoon salt

⅛ teaspoon ground red pepper

2 heads Belgian endive, leaves separated

If roasting your own peppers, preheat the oven to 425°F. Place the pepper halves, cut side down, on a baking sheet and bake, uncovered, until the skin is blackened, about 25 minutes. Place the peppers in a paper bag. Close the bag and let stand for 10 minutes. Scrape the charred skin from the peppers. (Alternately, you can roast the peppers by holding whole peppers with tongs over a gas flame or by placing them under the broiler and turning them until the skin blackens.)

Place the roasted peppers in a blender or food processor. Add the walnuts, garlic, tomato paste, oil, thyme, salt, and ground red pepper. Process until smooth and creamy. Transfer to a small bowl. Cover and refrigerate to firm slightly, about 30 minutes.

When ready to serve, spoon the pepper mixture into a pastry bag fitted with a large star tip. Pipe into the Belgian endive spears. Arrange the filled endive spears decoratively on a platter in a circular pattern.

**SERVES 6**

Per serving: 100 calories, 6 g fat, 4 g protein, 11 g carbohydrates, 7 g fiber, 0 mg cholesterol, 275 mg sodium

# RUMAKI-INSPIRED STUFFED MUSHROOMS

*The tantalizing flavors and textures of the stuffing for these mushrooms were inspired by the traditional rumaki ingredients of water chestnuts, bacon, ginger, and soy sauce. Despite its Japanese name, rumaki is believed to have its origins in Hawaii and was made popular in the United States during the 1950s by Trader Vic's restaurant.*

- 8 ounces white mushrooms
- 1 tablespoon olive oil
- 1 teaspoon finely chopped fresh ginger
- ¼ cup chopped canned water chestnuts
- 2 tablespoons soy bacon bits
- 2 tablespoons sherry or port
- 1 tablespoon low-sodium tamari soy sauce

Remove the stems from the mushroom caps and chop them. Set aside the caps.

Heat the oil in a large skillet over medium heat. Add the chopped mushroom stems and cook until softened, about 3 minutes. Stir in the ginger, water chestnuts, bacon bits, sherry or port, and tamari. Cook, stirring occasionally, about 3 minutes.

Preheat the oven to 425°F. Stuff the mushroom caps with the filling and arrange them in a single layer in a lightly oiled shallow baking dish. Cover loosely with foil and bake until the mushrooms are tender, about 20 to 30 minutes.

**SERVES 4**

Per serving: 62 calories, 4 g fat, 3 g protein, 4 g carbohydrates, 1 g fiber, 0 mg cholesterol, 178 mg sodium

# MUSHROOMS STUFFED WITH SPINACH AND PINE NUTS

*The wonderful flavor combination of spinach, pine nuts, and garlic teams up as a delightful stuffing for mushrooms that you'll want to make for company and for yourself, too.*

**16 ounces white mushrooms**
**1 tablespoon olive oil**
**1 clove garlic, finely chopped**
**1 package (10 ounces) frozen chopped spinach, cooked and squeezed dry**
**¼ cup chopped pine nuts**
**Salt and freshly ground black pepper**

Preheat the oven to 400°F.

Remove the stems from the mushroom caps and finely chop them. Set aside the caps.

Heat the oil in a large skillet over medium heat. Add the garlic and cook until fragrant, about 30 seconds. Stir in the chopped mushroom stems, spinach, and pine nuts; cook for 2 minutes. Season with salt and pepper to taste and mix well.

Press some of the stuffing mixture inside each mushroom cap and arrange the caps in a single layer in a lightly oiled shallow baking dish. Cover loosely with foil and bake until the mushrooms are tender, 20 to 30 minutes.

**SERVES 6**

Per serving: 75 calories, 5 g fat, 4 g protein, 4 g carbohydrates, 2 g fiber, 0 mg cholesterol, 32 mg sodium

# JERK-SPICED TEMPEH SKEWERS WITH MUSHROOMS AND BELL PEPPERS

*Instead of broiling, you may grill or roast these skewers in a hot oven and add additional vegetables if you like. If using wooden skewers, soak them in cold water for about 30 minutes so they won't burn.*

2 cloves garlic, crushed

2 scallions, coarsely chopped

1 tablespoon olive oil

1 tablespoon low-sodium tamari soy sauce

2 teaspoons fresh lime juice

1½ teaspoons ground allspice

1 teaspoon grated fresh ginger

½ teaspoon agave syrup

½ teaspoon dried thyme

¼ teaspoon freshly ground black pepper

¼ teaspoon ground cloves

¼ teaspoon ground red pepper

Salt

1 package (8 ounces) tempeh, cut into 1" pieces

1 red or yellow bell pepper, cut into 1" squares

6 ounces small mushroom caps

In a blender or small food processor, combine the garlic, scallions, oil, tamari, lime juice, allspice, ginger, agave syrup, thyme, black pepper, cloves, ground red pepper, and salt to taste. Process until smooth. Set aside.

Preheat the broiler with the top rack in the center of the oven. Place the tempeh in a saucepan of simmering water and cook for 10 minutes. Drain well, pat dry, and place in a shallow bowl. Coat the tempeh with the reserved spice mixture and thread onto wooden or metal skewers, alternating with pieces of the bell pepper and mushrooms. Place the skewers on a lightly oiled baking sheet and broil until browned, turning once, 10 to 15 minutes.

**SERVES 4**

Per serving: 154 calories, 6 g fat, 14 g protein, 11 g carbohydrates, 5 g fiber, 0 mg cholesterol, 162 mg sodium

## VEGETABLES UNDER FIRE

In addition to the bell peppers and mushrooms used in the Jerk-Spiced Tempeh Skewers, numerous other vegetables are terrific under (or over) fire. Next time you want to broil, roast, or grill veggies, try some of these: fennel, onion, zucchini, eggplant, tomatoes, cauliflower, radicchio, and asparagus. All of these vegetables, except for asparagus and radicchio, do well when cut into ½-inch slices. Asparagus should remain intact, with just the bottoms trimmed. Radicchio should be halved lengthwise.

# CAPONATA-TOPPED BAKED TOFU TRIANGLES

*This southern Italian eggplant salad is a flavorful topping for the baked tofu and is substantial enough to serve as an entrée. The caponata should be made ahead of time to let the flavors intensify.*

2 tablespoons olive oil

½ cup finely chopped onion

1 eggplant, peeled and chopped

2 cloves garlic, finely chopped

1 red bell pepper, chopped

1 cup diced canned tomatoes

Salt and freshly ground black pepper

2 tablespoons chopped black olives

2 tablespoons capers, rinsed, drained, and chopped

1 teaspoon red wine vinegar

1 tablespoon finely chopped fresh flat-leaf parsley

1 pound extra-firm tofu, drained and cut into ¼" slices

1 tablespoon low-sodium tamari soy sauce

Heat 1 tablespoon of the oil in a large skillet over medium heat. Add the onion, cover, and cook until soft, about 5 minutes. Stir in the eggplant. Cook, stirring occasionally, until the eggplant begins to soften. Add the garlic, bell pepper, tomatoes, and salt and pepper to taste. Cover and cook until the vegetables soften but still hold some shape, about 15 minutes.

Stir in the olives, capers, vinegar, and parsley. Taste to adjust the seasoning. Transfer to a bowl and cool to room temperature. (Make ahead to this point and refrigerate, if desired; bring the caponata back to room temperature before serving.)

Preheat the oven to 400°F. Lightly brush both sides of tofu with the remaining 1 tablespoon oil and the tamari. Cut each of the tofu slices diagonally to create two triangles each and place them on a baking sheet. Bake until lightly browned, turning once, 7 to 8 minutes per side. Remove from the oven and arrange on a platter. Top with the caponata and serve at once.

**SERVES 6**

Per serving: 133 calories, 8 g fat, 7 g protein, 11 g carbohydrates, 3 g fiber, 0 mg cholesterol, 239 mg sodium

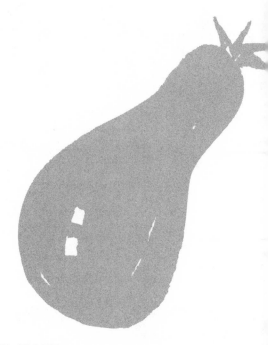

# VERY VEGETABLE SUSHI ROLLS

*Nori seaweed sheets, wasabi powder, and pickled ginger are available at well-stocked super-markets as well as natural food stores and Asian markets.*

3¼ cups water

½ cup wild rice

1¼ cups short-grain brown rice

½ teaspoon salt

1 tablespoon rice vinegar

6 roasted nori sheets

2 tablespoons toasted sesame seeds

Assorted vegetables for filling (see note)

1 tablespoon wasabi powder

1 tablespoon warm water

2 tablespoons pickled ginger

Low-sodium tamari soy sauce

In a medium saucepan, combine 3¼ cups water, wild rice, brown rice, and salt. Cover and bring to a boil. Reduce the heat to low and simmer until tender, about 45 minutes. Let stand, covered, for 5 minutes.

While the rice is still warm, transfer it to a wide, shallow bowl and spread it evenly with a large wooden spoon or a rice paddle. Sprinkle on the vinegar and set aside to cool.

Place 1 nori sheet on a bamboo sushi mat or a cloth napkin directly in front of you. Spread up to ½ cup of the rice mixture evenly over the nori sheet to the edge on the sides and close to the edge on the bottom and top. Sprinkle about 1 teaspoon sesame seeds over the rice. At the edge nearest to you, place at least 2 strips of vegetable filling ingredients on top of the rice.

Roll up the mat, beginning at the edge nearest you, pressing firmly against the nori. Once the nori is rolled up, wet the exposed top edge of the nori with a little water to seal the roll. Carefully press the mat around the sushi roll, then remove the mat. Cut the sushi roll into 6 pieces, using a sharp knife. Place the sushi pieces on their ends on a large platter. Repeat with the remaining ingredients.

Combine the wasabi powder with the warm water in a small bowl to make a paste. Place a small mound of the wasabi paste on the sushi platter, and garnish with a small pile of pickled ginger. Serve with small dipping bowls containing tamari. Sushi is best if eaten soon after its assembly, so make it close to serving time.

**SERVES 10**

Per serving: 127 calories, 2 g fat, 3 g protein, 25 g carbohydrates, 2 g fiber, 0 mg cholesterol, 190 mg sodium

Note: Among the choices for vegetable fillings are cooked thin asparagus spears and strips of avocado, cucumber, and red or yellow bell pepper. Strips of seitan and baked marinated tofu are also good filling choices.

## COOKING TIPS

• Roasting vegetables brings out their natural sweetness.

• Quick-cooking methods, such as steaming and stir-frying, preserve the texture and nutrients of vegetables.

• Fresh herbs and seasonings add sparkle to meals.

• Cooking fruits and vegetables in their skins helps to preserve fiber and nutrients.

# CHAPTER THREE

# SOUPED-UP SOUPS AND SIMMERING STEWS

Soups can provide versatility at mealtime. Whether enjoyed as a first course or the main event, soups made with fresh vegetables, beans, and legumes are nourishing ways to fill you up with healthy ingredients. The cuisines of the world inspired many of the recipes in this chapter that feature vegetables and beans low on the glycemic index.

The chapter begins with low-carb vegetable stock. If you prefer to use commercial broth, be sure to check the label, since some are fairly high in carbohydrates and sodium. In this chapter you'll find delightful clear-broth soups chock-full of vegetables as well as creamy pureed bisques and hearty chilies and stews. With this many choices, you'll surely find many satisfying ways to fill your family's soup bowls.

# LOW-CARB VEGETABLE STOCK

*Vegetable stock adds flavor and nutrients to soups, stews, and other recipes. You can also buy vegetable broth in cans or containers, or you can reconstitute powdered vegetable base or bouillon cubes. If you prefer to use a commercial vegetable broth, be sure to read the labels—some are higher in carbs and sodium than others.*

1 tablespoon olive oil

1 small onion, coarsely chopped

1 small carrot, cut into 1" pieces

2 ribs celery, coarsely chopped

1 cup chopped green beans

6 white mushrooms, halved

1 zucchini, coarsely chopped

2 cloves garlic, unpeeled and crushed

1/3 cup coarsely chopped fresh flat-leaf parsley

2 bay leaves

1/2 teaspoon black peppercorns

8 cups water

1 tablespoon low-sodium tamari soy sauce

1 teaspoon salt

Heat the oil in a large pot over medium heat. Add the onion, carrot, and celery and cook for 5 minutes. Stir in the beans, mushrooms, zucchini, garlic, parsley, bay leaves, and peppercorns. Add the water, tamari, and salt and bring to a boil. Reduce the heat to low and simmer, partially covered, for 1½ hours.

Cool slightly, then strain the stock through a fine-mesh sieve into a pot or bowl, pressing the vegetables against the sieve to release their juices. Store the cooled stock in tightly sealed containers in the refrigerator or freezer.

Properly stored, the stock will keep in the refrigerator for 3 to 5 days or in the freezer for up to 3 months.

**MAKES ABOUT 7 CUPS**

Per 1 cup: 55 calories, 3 g fat, 1 g protein, 6 g carbohydrates, 1 g fiber, 0 mg cholesterol, 537 mg sodium

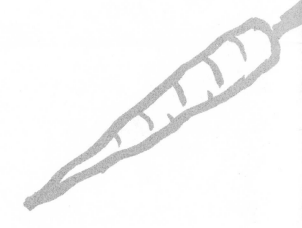

# OLD-FASHIONED VEGETABLE SOUP

*A classic, comforting vegetable soup can be enjoyed as a first course at dinner or as the main dish for a light supper or lunch. Vary the vegetables according to preference and availability.*

1 tablespoon olive oil

½ cup chopped onion

2 ribs celery, chopped

1 small carrot, chopped

1 clove garlic, finely chopped

1 small red bell pepper, chopped

6 ounces green beans, cut into 1" pieces

2 cups chopped cabbage

6 cups vegetable stock

1½ cups cooked dark red kidney beans

1 cup sliced white mushrooms

1–2 zucchini or yellow summer squash, halved lengthwise and cut into ¼" slices

Salt and freshly ground black pepper

2 tablespoons chopped fresh flat-leaf parsley

Heat the oil in a large pot over medium heat. Add the onion, celery, carrot, and garlic. Cover and cook until softened, about 3 minutes. Add the bell pepper, green beans, and cabbage and cook for 5 minutes. Add the stock, increase the heat to high, and bring to a boil. Reduce the heat to low and add the kidney beans, mushrooms, and zucchini or squash. Season to taste with salt and pepper. Simmer the soup until the vegetables are tender and the flavor has developed, about 30 minutes. Add the parsley and taste to adjust the seasoning.

SERVES 6

Per serving: 145 calories, 3 g fat, 6 g protein, 24 g carbohydrates, 8 g fiber, 0 mg cholesterol, 488 mg sodium

## MISO SOUP WITH BOK CHOY, SNOW PEAS, AND SHIITAKE MUSHROOMS

*Miso paste is a popular Japanese ingredient made from fermented soybeans, often in combination with other ingredients such as rice, barley, or chickpeas. In addition to its use in soups, miso paste can be used to season sauces, salad dressings, and main dishes. For a more substantial soup, add 8 ounces of diced firm tofu just before serving.*

5 cups water

1 cup finely shredded bok choy

6 small shiitake mushroom caps, thinly sliced

8–12 snow peas, cut diagonally into ½" pieces

2 scallions, chopped

1 tablespoon low-sodium tamari soy sauce

¼ cup white miso paste

Bring the water to a boil in a large saucepan. Add the bok choy, mushrooms, snow peas, scallions, and tamari. Reduce the heat to medium and simmer until the vegetables soften, about 5 minutes. Reduce the heat to low. Place the miso paste in a small bowl and stir in about ¼ cup of the hot soup, blending well. Add the blended miso mixture back into the soup and simmer for 2 to 3 minutes. Do not boil. Taste to adjust the seasoning.

**SERVES 4**

Per serving: 62 calories, 1 g fat, 3 g protein, 12 g carbohydrates, 2 g fiber, 0 mg cholesterol, 645 mg sodium

# THREE-BEAN MINESTRONE SOUP

*If yellow wax beans are unavailable, you can substitute another vegetable such as yellow summer squash or add a little extra of the other vegetables to make up the volume.*

1 tablespoon olive oil

½ cup chopped onion

½ cup chopped celery

¼ cup chopped carrot

2 cloves garlic, finely chopped

1½ cups green beans, cut into 1" pieces

1½ cups yellow wax beans, cut into 1" pieces

6 cups vegetable stock

Salt and freshly ground black pepper

1–2 zucchini, finely chopped

1½ cups cooked kidney beans

2 tablespoons finely chopped fresh flat-leaf parsley

1 tablespoon finely chopped fresh basil or 1 teaspoon dried basil

¼ teaspoon dried oregano

Grated soy Parmesan cheese

Heat the oil in a large pot over medium heat. Add the onion, celery, carrot, and garlic. Cover and cook until softened, about 5 minutes. Add the green beans, yellow beans, stock, and salt and pepper to taste. Bring to a boil, then reduce the heat to low and simmer for 20 minutes. Stir in the zucchini, kidney beans, parsley, dried basil (if using), and oregano; cook for another 15 minutes. Just before serving, stir in the fresh basil (if using). Ladle into bowls and garnish with soy Parmesan cheese.

**SERVES 6**

Per serving: 141 calories, 3 g fat, 6 g protein, 23 g carbohydrates, 8 g fiber, 0 mg cholesterol, 474 mg sodium

**Variation:** Grated regular Parmesan cheese may be used instead of the soy Parmesan.

# HOT-AND-SOUR SOUP WITH WATERCRESS, GINGER, AND WATER CHESTNUTS

*This fresh-tasting interpretation of hot-and-sour soup is loaded with delicious vegetables, tofu, and flavorful seasonings.*

1 tablespoon canola oil

8 ounces extra-firm tofu, cut into matchstick strips

1 tablespoon finely chopped fresh ginger

1 clove garlic, finely chopped

3 shiitake mushrooms, stems removed and caps cut into matchsticks

4½ cups vegetable stock

3 tablespoons rice vinegar

2 tablespoons low-sodium tamari soy sauce

1 teaspoon Asian chili paste

1 small bunch watercress, stemmed and chopped

1 can (8 ounces) bamboo shoots, drained, rinsed, and cut into matchsticks

¼ cup canned sliced water chestnuts, cut into matchsticks

1 tablespoon chopped scallions

Salt and freshly ground black pepper

1 tablespoon toasted sesame oil

Heat the canola oil in a large pot over medium-high heat. Add the tofu and cook until golden brown, about 5 minutes. Remove the tofu with a slotted spoon and set aside.

Add the ginger, garlic, and mushrooms to the pot and cook until fragrant, about 30 seconds. Stir in the stock, vinegar, tamari, and chili paste and bring to a boil. Reduce the heat to medium and simmer until the mushrooms are tender and the flavors have blended, about 5 minutes. Add the watercress, bamboo shoots, water chestnuts, scallions, and salt and pepper to taste. Stir in the reserved tofu and cook 5 minutes longer to heat through. Stir in the sesame oil.

**SERVES 4**

Per serving: 173 calories, 10 g fat, 8 g protein, 15 g carbohydrates, 4 g fiber, 0 mg cholesterol, 902 mg sodium

# TOM YUMMM! THAI-INSPIRED SOUP

*Inspired by the flavorful tom yum soup I've enjoyed in Thai restaurants, this version uses ingredients that can be found in most supermarkets. If oyster mushrooms are unavailable, sliced regular button mushrooms may be used.*

5 cups vegetable stock

1 piece (4") lemongrass, crushed

1 slice (¼") fresh ginger, peeled

Grated peel and juice of 1 lime

1 teaspoon Asian chili paste, or to taste

1 cup oyster mushrooms, quartered if large

16 pencil-thin asparagus spears, cut diagonally into 1" pieces

3 shallots, cut lengthwise into thin slivers

1 tablespoon low-sodium tamari soy sauce

3 scallions, chopped

2 tablespoons chopped fresh cilantro

In a large pot, combine the stock, lemongrass, ginger, about 1 teaspoon lime peel, and chili paste. Bring to a boil, then reduce the heat to low, cover, and simmer for 20 minutes. Strain the mixture through a sieve, return the broth to a saucepan, and bring to a boil. Add the mushrooms, asparagus, shallots, and tamari. Reduce the heat to low, cover, and cook for 3 minutes. Stir in the scallions and 1 tablespoon lime juice, or more to taste, and simmer until heated through, 1 to 2 minutes. Sprinkle with cilantro.

**SERVES 4**

Per serving: 78 calories, 1 g fat, 5 g protein, 13 g carbohydrates, 4 g fiber, 0 mg cholesterol, 805 mg sodium

# CLEAR MUSHROOM-LEEK SOUP WITH CELERY AND VERMOUTH

*Dry vermouth adds a sophisticated nuance to this flavorful soup made with juicy mushrooms, leeks, and slivers of refreshing celery.*

1 tablespoon olive oil

2 leeks, white part only, well washed and chopped

2–3 ribs celery, including leaves, chopped

6 cups vegetable stock

2½ tablespoons dry vermouth

2 bay leaves

12 ounces white mushrooms, sliced

2 tablespoons finely chopped fresh flat-leaf parsley

Salt and freshly ground black pepper

Heat the oil in a large pot over medium heat. Add the leeks and celery. Cover and cook until softened, about 5 minutes. Add the stock, vermouth, and bay leaves and simmer, covered, for 15 minutes. Stir in the mushrooms and parsley. Season with salt and pepper to taste and cook 10 minutes longer, or until the mushrooms are tender. Remove and discard the bay leaves before serving.

**SERVES 4**

Per serving: 142 calories, 4 g fat, 6 g protein, 19 g carbohydrates, 4 g fiber, 0 mg cholesterol, 725 mg sodium

# THREE-GREENS SOUP

*Dark leafy greens are bursting with nutrients and are naturally low in carbs, giving you two good reasons to enjoy this soup. Another reason to enjoy it is, of course, because it tastes terrific.*

4 cups vegetable stock

1 clove garlic, finely chopped

1 bunch scallions, chopped

2 cups coarsely chopped escarole

2 cups coarsely chopped spinach

2 cups coarsely chopped leaf lettuce

1 teaspoon fresh lemon juice

1 tablespoon finely chopped fresh basil, savory, or tarragon

Pinch of ground nutmeg

Salt and freshly ground black pepper

In a large pot, combine the stock, garlic, and scallions and bring to a boil. Reduce the heat to medium and stir in the escarole. Cover and cook for 10 minutes. Stir in the spinach and leaf lettuce, cover, and cook 5 minutes. Use an immersion blender to puree the soup (or transfer to a blender or food processor in batches). When ready to serve, reheat the soup and stir in the lemon juice, herb, nutmeg, and salt and pepper to taste.

SERVES 4

Per serving: 73 calories, 1 g fat, 2 g protein, 14 g carbohydrates, 6 g fiber, 0 mg cholesterol, 520 mg sodium

# SUMMER VEGETABLE BISQUE

*Here's a healthful way to cut the fat and cholesterol out of cream soups: Omit the cream. Instead, puree the vegetables and the stock into a creamy full-flavored soup.*

1 tablespoon olive oil

½ cup chopped onion

½ cup chopped celery

¼ cup chopped carrot

1 small yellow bell pepper, chopped

1 zucchini, chopped

1 yellow summer squash, chopped

4 ounces white mushrooms, chopped

4 ounces green beans, cut into 1" pieces

1 cucumber, peeled, seeded, and chopped

3 cups vegetable stock

1 tablespoon chopped fresh flat-leaf parsley

1 tablespoon finely chopped fresh savory, basil, or tarragon or 1 teaspoon dried

Salt and freshly ground black pepper

Heat the oil in a large pot over medium heat. Add the onion, celery, carrot, and bell pepper. Cover and cook until softened, about 5 minutes. Add the zucchini, squash, mushrooms, beans, cucumber, stock, parsley, and herb; simmer until the vegetables are tender, about 15 minutes. Use an immersion blender to puree the soup (or transfer to a blender or food processor in batches). Season with salt and pepper to taste.

**SERVES 4**

Per serving: 99 calories, 4 g fat, 3 g protein, 14 g carbohydrates, 4 g fiber, 0 mg cholesterol, 351 mg sodium

# SPICY PORTUGUESE KALE SOUP

*For a heartier soup, sauté thin slices of vegetarian sausage links and add them to the soup when ready to serve.*

1 tablespoon olive oil

½ cup chopped onion

1 clove garlic, finely chopped

5 cups vegetable stock

3½ cups chopped kale

1 tablespoon low-sodium tamari soy sauce

¼ teaspoon red-pepper flakes, or to taste

1 bay leaf

Salt

1 cup cooked white beans

2 tablespoons chopped fresh flat-leaf parsley

1 teaspoon fresh marjoram or ½ teaspoon dried marjoram

Heat the oil in a large pot over medium heat. Add the onion and garlic, cover, and cook until softened, about 3 minutes. Add the stock, kale, tamari, red-pepper flakes, bay leaf, and salt to taste and bring to a boil. Reduce the heat to medium, add the beans, and cook until the vegetables are tender, about 30 minutes. About 10 minutes before serving, stir in the parsley and marjoram. Remove and discard the bay leaf.

SERVES 4

Per serving: 157 calories, 5 g fat, 8 g protein, 26 g carbohydrates, 6 g fiber, 0 mg cholesterol, 754 mg sodium

# ARTICHOKE EDAMAME BISQUE

*Save time by using frozen artichokes and shelled edamame for this luscious soup that has a creamy green color with the consistency of potato-leek soup. This is one you'll want to make for company.*

    1 tablespoon olive oil

    ½ cup chopped onion

    ⅓ cup chopped celery

    4 cups vegetable stock, or more

    2 packages (10 ounces each) frozen artichoke hearts

    1½ cups fresh or frozen shelled edamame

    1 bay leaf

    Salt

    Ground red pepper

Heat the oil in a large pot over medium heat. Add the onion and celery, cover, and cook until softened, about 5 minutes. Add 4 cups stock, artichokes, edamame, bay leaf, salt to taste, and ground red pepper to taste. Bring to a boil, then reduce the heat to low and simmer, covered, until the vegetables are tender, 20 to 30 minutes. Remove and discard the bay leaf. Using a slotted spoon, retrieve several edamame to use as a garnish.

Use an immersion blender to puree the soup (or transfer to a blender or food processor in batches). Add more stock if the soup is too thick and taste to adjust the seasoning.

For a silkier consistency, strain the soup through a fine-mesh sieve before serving. Ladle the soup into bowls and garnish with the reserved edamame.

**SERVES 6**

Per serving: 181 calories, 7 g fat, 12 g protein, 20 g carbohydrates, 10 g fiber, 0 mg cholesterol, 366 mg sodium

# CREAMY DOUBLE CELERY SOUP

*This rich creamy soup will give you a new appreciation for celery, an often unappreciated vegetable. It's paired here with its flavor cousin, celeriac (celery root).*

1 tablespoon olive oil

1 small onion, chopped

3 ribs celery, tough strings removed, chopped

1 celeriac, peeled and chopped

4 cups vegetable stock

Salt and freshly ground black pepper

Heat the oil in a large pot over medium heat. Add the onion, celery, and celeriac. Cover and cook until the vegetables are softened, about 10 minutes. Add the stock and bring to a boil. Reduce the heat to low, season with salt and pepper to taste, and simmer until the vegetables are tender, about 30 minutes. Use an immersion blender to puree the soup (or transfer to a blender or food processor in batches). Ladle into bowls and garnish with chopped celery leaves.

SERVES 4

Per serving: 124 calories, 5 g fat, 4 g protein, 18 g carbohydrates, 5 g fiber, 0 mg cholesterol, 582 mg sodium

**Variation:** Add ¼ cup heavy cream for extra richness.

## THOUGHT FOR FOOD

Certain groups of people in the world consume 65 percent and more of their calories from carbohydrates, yet they have the lowest rates of obesity and chronic disease. The carbohydrates they eat are almost exclusively derived from whole plant foods rather than refined processed foods. This illustrates that the source of the carbohydrates is more important than the percentage of calories from the carbs.

# ASPARAGUS AND OYSTER MUSHROOM BISQUE

*This sumptuously elegant soup is deceptively simple to make—it's a great first course for a special meal.*

4 teaspoons olive oil

1 rib celery, chopped

1 leek, white part only, well washed and chopped

2 shallots, chopped

1 pound asparagus spears, cut into 1" lengths

3 cups vegetable stock

¼ cup white wine

Salt and freshly ground black pepper

8 ounces oyster mushrooms

1 teaspoon finely chopped fresh tarragon or ½ teaspoon dried tarragon

Heat 2 teaspoons of the oil in a large pot over medium heat. Add the celery, leek, shallots, and asparagus. Cover and cook until the vegetables begin to soften, stirring occasionally, about 5 minutes. Add the stock, wine, and salt and pepper to taste. Simmer until the vegetables are tender, about 15 minutes. With a slotted spoon, remove 4 to 8 asparagus tips and reserve for garnish.

Slice or quarter the larger mushrooms, leaving the smaller ones whole or halved. In a medium skillet, sauté the mushrooms in the remaining 2 teaspoons oil for 1 to 2 minutes. Set aside.

Stir one-fourth of the mushrooms into the soup. Use an immersion blender to puree the soup (or transfer to a blender or food processor in batches). Stir in the remaining mushrooms and the tarragon. Cook over medium heat until hot, 3 to 5 minutes, stirring occasionally. Ladle into bowls and garnish with the reserved asparagus tips.

**SERVES 4**

Per serving: 138 calories, 5 g fat, 8 g protein, 15 g carbohydrates, 4 g fiber, 0 mg cholesterol, 391 mg sodium

# SPICY CREOLE GUMBO WITH COLLARDS

*Gumbo and collards are two mainstays of Southern cooking, so it seemed only natural to combine them in this zesty brew. The collards are precooked separately to prevent any of their bitterness from finding its way into the gumbo. The optional filé powder (ground sassafras leaves) is worth locating; it lends an authentic flavor to the gumbo. Look for it at gourmet grocers and larger supermarkets.*

> 1 bunch collards, coarsely chopped
>
> 1 tablespoon olive oil
>
> ½ cup finely chopped onion
>
> 1 green bell pepper, chopped
>
> ¾ cup thinly sliced celery
>
> 2 cloves garlic, finely chopped
>
> 1 cup diced tomatoes
>
> 1 teaspoon dried thyme
>
> 1 teaspoon filé powder (optional)
>
> 6 cups vegetable stock
>
> Salt and freshly ground black pepper
>
> 1 cup cooked kidney beans or other red beans
>
> 1 teaspoon Tabasco, or to taste

Cook the collards in a pot of boiling salted water just until tender, 5 to 7 minutes. Drain and set aside.

Heat the oil in a large pot over medium heat. Add the onion, bell pepper, celery, and garlic and cook, covered, for 5 minutes, or until soft, stirring occasionally. Stir in the tomatoes, thyme, and filé powder (if using). Add the stock and salt and pepper to taste. Simmer over low heat for 30 minutes, stirring occasionally.

Stir in the reserved collards, beans, and Tabasco. Taste to adjust the seasoning and cook 10 to 15 minutes longer.

**SERVES 6**

Per serving: 147 calories, 3 g fat, 7 g protein, 24 g carbohydrates, 9 g fiber, 0 mg cholesterol, 528 mg sodium

## BETTER BEANS

For convenience, many of the recipes using cooked beans call for 1½ cups, which is the equivalent of one 15-to-16-ounce can of drained beans.

Home-cooked dried beans are lower in sodium than canned beans, but if you do buy canned beans, buy organic. They are low in sodium in addition to having other health benefits that come from being organic.

# HEARTS OF PALM SOUP WITH ASPARAGUS AND LEEKS

*The luxurious ingredients in this soup signal the start of a special meal. No one would guess by the rich flavor how simple it is to put together.*

    1 tablespoon olive oil
    1 leek, white part only, well washed and chopped
    1 pound asparagus spears, coarsely chopped
    4 cups vegetable stock
    1 can (14½ ounces) hearts of palm, drained, rinsed, and cut into 1" pieces
    ½ teaspoon salt
    Freshly ground black pepper
    Finely chopped fresh flat-leaf parsley

Heat the oil in a large pot over medium heat. Add the leek, cover, and cook until softened, about 3 minutes. Stir in the asparagus and cook 3 minutes longer. Add the stock, hearts of palm, salt, and pepper to taste; bring to a boil. Reduce the heat to low and simmer, covered, for 20 minutes. Use an immersion blender to puree the soup (or transfer to a blender or food processor in batches). Taste to adjust the seasoning. Ladle into bowls and garnish with parsley.

**SERVES 4**

Per serving: 122 calories, 5 g fat, 7 g protein, 16 g carbohydrates, 5 g fiber, 0 mg cholesterol, 946 mg sodium

**Variation:** Add a garnish of sour cream.

# SPLIT PEA SOUP WITH CABBAGE AND "BACON"

*As with many other soups and stews, the flavor of this split pea soup improves with time, so plan to make it a day ahead of when you need it. It will be nice and thick, yet light and delicious at the same time. In addition to the soy bacon bits, you might want to garnish the soup with a few slivers of radish for color and crunch.*

1 tablespoon olive oil

½ cup chopped onion

2 cups shredded Savoy cabbage

6 cups water

1½ cups dried green split peas

1 teaspoon finely chopped fresh savory or ½ teaspoon dried savory

2 bay leaves

Salt and freshly ground black pepper

Liquid smoke (optional)

Soy bacon bits

Heat the oil in a large pot over medium heat. Add the onion, cover, and cook until softened, about 3 minutes. Stir in the cabbage and cook 5 minutes longer. Add the water, split peas, savory, bay leaves, and salt and pepper to taste. Bring to a boil, then reduce the heat to low, cover, and cook until the vegetables are soft and the soup thickens, stirring occasionally, about 1 hour. Remove and discard the bay leaves. Add a dash of liquid smoke (if using). Ladle the soup into bowls and garnish with soy bacon bits.

**SERVES 6**

Per serving: 180 calories, 3 g fat, 11 g protein, 29 g carbohydrates, 11 g fiber, 0 mg cholesterol, 10 mg sodium

# TUSCAN WHITE BEAN AND ESCAROLE SOUP

*It's best to cook greens such as escarole before adding them to soup to remove any of their bitterness. Look for the largest head of escarole you can find—you may be surprised at how much it cooks down.*

1 large head escarole, coarsely chopped

1 tablespoon olive oil

½ cup finely chopped onion

2 cloves garlic, finely chopped

1½ cups cooked cannellini beans

5 cups vegetable stock

¼ teaspoon red-pepper flakes, or to taste

Salt and freshly ground black pepper

Cook the escarole in a pot of boiling salted water until slightly softened, about 5 minutes. Drain and set aside.

Heat the oil in a large pot over medium heat. Add the onion and cook until softened, about 3 minutes. Add the garlic and cook 1 minute longer. Stir in the beans, stock, reserved escarole, red-pepper flakes, and salt and pepper to taste. Simmer for 20 minutes to heat through and allow the flavors to develop.

## SERVES 4

Per serving: 167 calories, 5 g fat, 9 g protein, 29 g carbohydrates, 10 g fiber, 0 mg cholesterol, 604 mg sodium

# BLACK BEAN SOUP WITH LEMON GREMOLATA

*A sprinkling of gremolata—a zesty Milanese seasoning mixture of garlic, lemons, and parsley—adds color and piquancy to this flavorful and satisfying soup.*

3 cloves garlic, finely chopped

¼ cup chopped fresh flat-leaf parsley

Peel of 1 lemon, removed with a vegetable peeler

1 tablespoon olive oil

⅓ cup chopped onion

1 large red bell pepper, chopped

1 cup chopped celery

3 cups cooked black beans

6 cups water

1 bay leaf

1 teaspoon ground cumin

½ teaspoon dried oregano

Salt and freshly ground black pepper

Finely chop together 2 garlic cloves with the parsley and lemon peel until well combined to make the gremolata. Set aside.

Heat the oil in a large pot over medium heat. Add the onion, bell pepper, celery, and remaining 1 garlic clove. Cover and cook until softened, about 5 minutes. Stir in the beans, water, bay leaf, cumin, oregano, and salt and pepper to taste. Cover and cook until the vegetables are tender, about 1 hour. Remove and discard the bay leaf. Taste to adjust the seasoning.

Use an immersion blender to puree the soup (or transfer to a blender or food processor in batches). Serve sprinkled with the reserved gremolata.

**SERVES 6**

Per serving: 154 calories, 3 g fat, 8 g protein, 25 g carbohydrates, 9 g fiber, 0 mg cholesterol, 3 mg sodium

# MOROCCAN-SPICED LENTIL SOUP

*Fragrant spices transform everyday lentil soup into an exotic potage. Serve with a crisp green salad for a satisfying lunch or a light supper. Be sure to pick through the dried lentils first to remove any tiny stones or other debris and then rinse the lentils before using.*

1 tablespoon olive oil

½ cup chopped onion

1 clove garlic, chopped

1 small red bell pepper, chopped

1 teaspoon finely chopped fresh ginger

¼ teaspoon red-pepper flakes, or to taste

½ teaspoon ground cinnamon

½ teaspoon ground coriander

¼ teaspoon ground cumin

¼ teaspoon ground fennel seeds

¾ cup dried brown lentils

3 cups water

3 cups broth

Salt and freshly ground black pepper

Heat the oil in a large pot over medium heat. Add the onion and garlic. Cover and cook until slightly softened, about 5 minutes. Add the bell pepper, ginger, red-pepper flakes, cinnamon, coriander, cumin, and fennel; stir until fragrant, about 30 seconds. Add the lentils, water, broth, and salt and pepper to taste. Cover and cook until the lentils are soft, about 1 hour.

## SERVES 6

Per serving: 172 calories, 3 g fat, 11 g protein, 27 g carbohydrates, 10 g fiber, 0 mg cholesterol, 3 mg sodium

# JAMMIN' JAMBALAYA

*Jambalaya is traditionally served over white rice, but if you want to keep the carbs down and the nutrients up, try it over the Three-Rice Pilaf on page 130.*

1 tablespoon olive oil

1 cup chopped celery

½ cup chopped onion

1 large green bell pepper, chopped

1 small hot chile pepper, seeded and finely chopped

2 cloves garlic, finely chopped

1 cup diced canned tomatoes

1½ cups cooked dark red kidney beans

1 package (8 ounces) Lightlife Chick'n Strips, cut into ½" pieces (optional; see note)

1 cup water

1 teaspoon dried thyme

Salt and freshly ground black pepper

Tabasco, to taste

Heat the oil in a large saucepan over medium heat. Add the celery, onion, bell pepper, chile pepper (if using), and garlic. Cover and cook until softened, about 10 minutes. Stir in the tomatoes and cook 1 minute. Add the beans, Chick'n Strips (if using), water, thyme, and salt and pepper to taste. Simmer until the liquid cooks down and the flavors have blended, about 30 minutes. Add a splash of Tabasco and serve additional to be added according to individual taste.

## SERVES 4

Per serving: 162 calories, 4 g fat, 7 g protein, 27 g carbohydrates, 9 g fiber, 0 mg cholesterol, 111 mg sodium

Note: The optional Lightlife Chick'n Strips, available in large supermarkets and natural food stores, are low in carbs and add a meaty texture to this jambalaya. Sliced and browned veggie sausage links or seitan would also make a good addition at the end of cooking time. If you prefer not to use meat alternatives, additional vegetables or beans may be added to increase the volume of this dish.

# BOUNTIFUL "BIG BOWL" CHILI

*The red lentils help to make this a thick, almost creamy chili. A crisp green salad is an ideal accompaniment for taste and textural contrast.*

1 tablespoon olive oil

½ cup chopped onion

1 bell pepper (any color), chopped

1 clove garlic, finely chopped

1 small hot chile pepper, seeded and finely chopped

2 cups chopped white mushrooms

2–3 tablespoons chili powder

1 tablespoon tomato paste

¾ cup hot or mild tomato salsa

½ cup dried red lentils

1½ cups cooked kidney beans

2 cups water

½ teaspoon salt, or to taste

¼ teaspoon freshly ground black pepper

Heat the oil in a large pot over medium heat. Add the onion and bell pepper, cover, and cook until softened, stirring occasionally, about 5 minutes. Add the garlic, chile pepper, and mushrooms; cook until the mushrooms release their liquid, about 3 minutes. Stir in the chili powder, tomato paste, salsa, lentils, kidney beans, water, salt, and pepper. Simmer, partially covered, stirring occasionally, until the lentils are tender and the flavors are blended, about 30 minutes. Taste to adjust the seasoning.

**SERVES 4**

Per serving: 180 calories, 5 g fat, 9 g protein, 28 g carbohydrates, 7 g fiber, 0 mg cholesterol, 553 mg sodium

# CHILI CON VEGGIES

*No "carne" in this chili—just loads of low-carb veggies, including meaty eggplant, along with kidney beans and chili spices. For a mild version, omit the hot chile pepper.*

1 tablespoon olive oil

½ cup finely chopped onion

½ cup finely chopped celery

1 eggplant, peeled and chopped

1 red bell pepper, chopped

1 zucchini, chopped

1 small hot chile pepper, seeded and finely chopped

1 clove garlic, finely chopped

1 tablespoon tomato paste

2–3 tablespoons chili powder

1 tablespoon low-sodium tamari soy sauce

1½ cups cooked kidney beans

1½ cups water

Salt and freshly ground black pepper

Heat the oil in a large pot over medium heat. Add the onion and celery. Cover and cook until softened, about 5 minutes. Add the eggplant, bell pepper, zucchini, chile pepper, and garlic; cook until softened, stirring occasionally, about 10 minutes. Stir in the tomato paste, chili powder, tamari, kidney beans, water, and salt and pepper to taste. Simmer until the vegetables are tender, stirring occasionally, about 45 minutes.

## SERVES 4

Per serving: 135 calories, 3 g fat, 6 g protein, 23 g carbohydrates, 9 g fiber, 0 mg cholesterol, 337 mg sodium

# VICTORY GARDEN STEW

*A variety of fresh-picked vegetables are the inspiration for this flavorful stew. I used to add white potatoes to my stew and serve it with crusty white bread—now I serve it over a freshly cooked whole grain, usually quinoa, brown rice, or bulgur, for a satisfying good-carb meal.*

1 tablespoon olive oil

2 ribs celery, sliced

1 leek, white part only, well washed and coarsely chopped

1 small carrot, sliced

1 large fennel bulb, finely chopped

1 red bell pepper, chopped

6 ounces green beans, cut into 1" pieces

1 zucchini, halved and cut into ¼" slices

1 yellow summer squash, halved and cut into ¼" slices

1½ cups fresh or frozen shelled edamame

3½ cups water

1 teaspoon finely chopped fresh thyme or ½ teaspoon dried thyme

1 teaspoon salt

¼ teaspoon freshly ground black pepper

2 cups cooked chopped kale or other dark leafy greens

Heat the oil in a medium pot over medium heat. Add the celery, leek, and carrot. Cover and cook 5 minutes to soften slightly. Add the fennel, bell pepper, green beans, zucchini, squash, edamame, water, thyme, salt, and pepper. Cover and cook until the vegetables are tender and the flavors have blended, about 1 hour. For a thicker stew, puree up to 2 cups of the solids in a blender or food processor at this point. About 10 minutes before serving, stir in the cooked kale.

**SERVES 4**

Per serving: 188 calories, 7 g fat, 12 g protein, 23 g carbohydrates, 8 g fiber, 0 mg cholesterol, 747 mg sodium

# COOL-AS-A-CUCUMBER FENNEL SOUP

*When served cold, this light, delicious soup is perfect for a hot day—and so very easy to put together. But it tastes great warm or at room temperature, too, and looks lovely garnished with thinly sliced cucumber and chopped fennel fronds.*

2 teaspoons olive oil

1 clove garlic

1 leek, white part only, well washed and chopped

2 fennel bulbs, chopped plus some fronds for garnish

2 cups vegetable stock

¾ teaspoon salt

4 cucumbers, peeled, seeded, and chopped plus 12 very thin cucumber
   slices for garnish

1 tablespoon finely chopped fresh flat-leaf parsley

Heat the oil in a large pot over medium heat. Add the garlic and leek, cover, and cook until softened, about 3 minutes. Stir in the fennel, stock, and salt and bring to a boil. Reduce the heat to low, cover, and cook for 30 minutes.

Add the chopped cucumbers and parsley and cook 10 minutes longer. Use an immersion blender to puree the soup (or transfer to a blender or food processor in batches). Serve hot or cold. (If serving cold, transfer to a container and chill well.) Ladle the soup into bowls and garnish with the cucumber slices and a sprinkling of chopped fennel fronds.

**SERVES 4**

Per serving: 88 calories, 3 g fat, 2 g protein, 15 g carbohydrates, 5 g fiber, 0 mg cholesterol, 732 mg sodium

# CURRIED CAULIFLOWER VICHYSSOISE

*I decided that as long as I was already taking one liberty with vichyssoise by using cauliflower instead of potatoes, why not go further still and season it with curry? After all, cauliflower and curry are a wonderful match. Try this soup and see if you don't agree.*

1 tablespoon olive oil

2 leeks, white part only, well washed and chopped

1 tablespoon curry powder, or to taste

1 head cauliflower, coarsely chopped

3½ cups vegetable stock

1 teaspoon fresh lemon juice

½ cup soy milk

½ teaspoon salt

⅛ teaspoon ground red pepper

Chopped fresh flat-leaf parsley or chives

Heat the oil in a large pot over medium heat. Add the leeks and cook until soft, about 5 minutes. Stir in the curry powder, then add the cauliflower and the stock and simmer until the cauliflower is soft, about 20 minutes. Use an immersion blender to puree the soup (or transfer to a blender or food processor in batches). Transfer to a bowl or other container and stir in the lemon juice, soy milk, salt, and ground red pepper. Cover and refrigerate for several hours or overnight. Taste to adjust the seasoning. Ladle into bowls and garnish with parsley or chives.

**SERVES 4**

Per serving: 135 calories, 5 g fat, 5 g protein, 20 g carbohydrates, 6 g fiber, 0 mg cholesterol, 750 mg sodium

**Variation:** Regular dairy milk may be used instead of the soy milk.

# GARDEN-VARIETY GAZPACHO

*Celebrate summer. Enjoy loads of veggies from the garden—without heating up the kitchen.*

3 cucumbers, peeled, seeded, and chopped

1 large tomato, chopped

1 small red bell pepper, chopped

¼ cup chopped sweet yellow onion

1 small yellow bell pepper, chopped

⅓ cup finely chopped celery

1 clove garlic, finely chopped

1 hot or mild chile pepper, seeded and finely chopped

2 tablespoons chopped scallion

1 tablespoon capers, rinsed, drained, and chopped

2 tablespoons white wine vinegar

2 tablespoons olive oil

1 teaspoon salt

1 teaspoon Tabasco (optional)

2½ cups vegetable stock

2 tablespoons finely chopped fresh flat-leaf parsley plus additional for garnish

1 teaspoon fresh lemon juice (optional)

In a blender or food processor, combine 2 cucumbers, tomato, red bell pepper, and onion; process until smooth. Pour the vegetable mixture into a large bowl and stir in the remaining cucumber, yellow bell pepper, celery, garlic, chile pepper, scallion, and capers. Add the vinegar, oil, salt, and Tabasco (if using). Stir in the stock and the 2 tablespoons of parsley. Cover the bowl and refrigerate for at least 2 hours or overnight for the flavors to blend and for the soup to chill. Taste to adjust the seasoning, adding the lemon juice, if desired, to brighten the flavors. Serve the soup chilled and garnished with the remaining chopped parsley.

## SERVES 4

Per serving: 129 calories, 7 g fat, 3 g protein, 14 g carbohydrates, 4 g fiber, 0 mg cholesterol, 950 mg sodium

# CHAPTER FOUR

# HIGH-POWERED SALADS

Whether you're watching your weight or trying to eat healthy, salads are an important part of your diet. But facing that same bowl of lettuce day after day can get tiresome. Now is the time to rethink the salad—not just as an accompaniment to a meal but as the integral part of it.

When you employ a variety of beans, seeds, vegetables, and dressings, your main-dish salads can satisfy for both lunch and dinner. I especially like to pair soup and salad at a meal because each takes a while to eat and they contrast each other texturally. By the time you finish eating, you're full and satisfied. Plus, you can enjoy a large bowl of each without worrying about too many carbs or calories or too much fat.

Among the main-dish salads to choose from in this chapter are Tabbouleh-Style Quinoa Salad, Tempeh-Walnut Salad with Lime and Cilantro, and Chopped Vegetable Salad with Baked Tofu. There are also plenty of side salads, such as Sesame Coleslaw with Daikon, Snow Peas, and Ginger; and Moroccan Green Pepper Salad. Turn salad into a hearty low-carb sandwich with Soy-Good "Egg" Salad or Ragin' Cajun Tastes-like-Chicken Salad wrapped in a lettuce leaf or spread on whole grain or other low-carb bread. And if you're looking for a salad to serve with a special meal, consider Green Goodness Salad, Four-of-Hearts Salad, or sumptuous Fennel Salad with Sun-Dried Tomatoes, Black Olives, and Pine Nuts.

# INDONESIAN-STYLE TEMPEH AND VEGETABLE SALAD

*Tempeh is the name for compressed soybean cakes that originated in Indonesia. Hot chili paste, called* sambal oelek, *is available at Asian groceries and large supermarkets.*

2 tablespoons toasted sesame oil

1 tablespoon rice vinegar

1 tablespoon low-sodium tamari soy sauce

1 teaspoon Asian chili paste, or to taste

2 cups crumbled poached tempeh (see note)

3 cups shredded iceberg lettuce or green cabbage

1 cup snow peas, blanched

¼ cup canned sliced water chestnuts

¼ cup grated carrot

2 scallions, chopped

2 tablespoons canola oil

1 clove garlic, finely chopped

1 tablespoon fresh lemon juice

1 teaspoon grated fresh ginger

1 cup bean sprouts, blanched

¼ cup chopped roasted peanuts

In a shallow bowl, combine the sesame oil, vinegar, tamari, and chili paste. Add the tempeh and toss to coat well. Cover and refrigerate for several hours or overnight.

In a large bowl, combine the lettuce or cabbage, snow peas, water chestnuts, carrot, and scallions. In a small bowl combine the canola oil, garlic, lemon juice, and ginger; drizzle over the vegetables. Toss well to combine. Add the marinated tempeh with its dressing and toss well. Serve sprinkled with the bean sprouts and peanuts.

## SERVES 4

Per serving: 401 calories, 28 g fat, 22 g protein, 22 g carbohydrates, 5 g fiber, 0 mg cholesterol, 387 mg sodium

Note: Poaching tempeh mellows its flavor. Place the tempeh in a saucepan, cover with water, and simmer for 10 minutes. Drain and pat dry before using.

# BOUNTIFUL VEGGIE CHEF SALAD

*Strips of veggie ham and baked tofu make this a hearty protein-rich main-dish salad that is low in carbs and fat, with zero cholesterol. There are a number of brands of veggie deli slices available. One brand that can be found in many supermarkets is Lightlife Smart Deli slices (I like the Country Ham Style). Four slices contain 5 grams of carbohydrates, 1 gram of fiber, and 16 grams of protein, with zero fat and zero cholesterol—now that's my kind of ham!*

1 clove garlic, chopped

½ teaspoon mustard powder

½ teaspoon dried basil

½ teaspoon salt

Freshly ground black pepper

3 tablespoons white wine vinegar

½ cup olive oil

8–12 cups torn mixed salad greens

6 ounces vegetable ham slices, cut into ½" strips

1 package (8 ounces) baked tofu, cut into ½" strips

4 cherry tomatoes, halved

½ cucumber, peeled, seeded, and thinly sliced

8 pitted kalamata olives

4 red radishes, chopped

In a blender or food processor, blend the garlic, mustard, basil, salt, pepper to taste, and vinegar. Add the oil and blend until emulsified. Set aside.

Divide the lettuce among individual shallow salad bowls. Arrange the strips of ham and baked tofu on top of each salad in a circular pattern. Place cherry tomatoes, cucumber slices, and olives on each salad in between the ham and tofu. Sprinkle with the radishes. Drizzle each salad with some of the reserved dressing.

**SERVES 4**

Per serving: 383 calories, 32 g fat, 15 g protein, 10 g carbohydrates, 3 g fiber, 0 mg cholesterol, 637 mg sodium

# CHOPPED VEGETABLE SALAD WITH BAKED TOFU

*This is a substantial salad with lots of goodies that are attractive, delicious, and easy to assemble. The dressing is ideal for virtually any green salad, so consider making extra for other salads. Commercially prepared baked tofu is widely available in natural food stores and larger supermarkets.*

⅓ cup olive oil

3 tablespoons cider vinegar

1 tablespoon Dijon mustard

1 tablespoon finely chopped fresh flat-leaf parsley

1 teaspoon finely chopped garlic

1 tablespoon chopped scallion

Salt and freshly ground black pepper

½ small head Boston lettuce, torn into bite-size pieces

½ small head red or green leaf lettuce, torn into bite-size pieces

1 English cucumber, peeled, halved lengthwise, and chopped

6 radishes, chopped

½ cup chopped red bell pepper

½ cup chopped celery

4 canned artichoke hearts, chopped

1 tomato, chopped

1 package (8 ounces) baked tofu, cut into ½" cubes

In a blender or food processor, blend the oil, vinegar, mustard, parsley, garlic, scallion, and salt and pepper to taste. Set aside.

Place the Boston and leaf lettuce in a serving bowl. Add the cucumber, radishes, bell pepper, celery, artichoke hearts, tomato, and tofu. Drizzle on the reserved dressing and toss to combine.

**SERVES 4**

Per serving: 253 calories, 20 g fat, 7 g protein, 13 g carbohydrates, 3 g fiber, 0 mg cholesterol, 362 mg sodium

# TEMPEH-WALNUT SALAD WITH LIME AND CILANTRO

*This is a wonderful combination of textures and flavors that will have you sneaking tastes right out of the mixing bowl before serving time. Diced avocado, used judiciously because of its high (but good-for-you) fat content, would be a wonderful addition—one small avocado divided among four salads keeps the fat to a minimum but adds a lot of great taste and texture. The tempeh is poached in simmering water for 10 minutes prior to using in recipes to mellow the flavor and aid in digestion.*

2 tablespoons soy mayonnaise

3 tablespoons olive oil

2½ tablespoons fresh lime peel

1 teaspoon grated lime peel

Salt

Tabasco

1½ cups poached tempeh (see note), diced

½ cup walnut pieces, lightly toasted

5 cups torn mixed salad greens

1 small carrot, shredded

8 cherry tomatoes, halved

2 tablespoons black olive halves

2 tablespoons chopped fresh cilantro

Freshly ground black pepper

In a small bowl, whisk together the mayonnaise, 2 tablespoons oil, 2 tablespoons lime juice, lime peel, ½ teaspoon salt, and Tabasco to taste. Stir in the tempeh and walnuts and set aside.

In a large bowl, combine the greens, carrot, tomatoes, olives, and cilantro. Drizzle on the remaining 1 tablespoon oil and ½ tablespoon lime juice, and season with salt and pepper to taste. Toss gently to combine. Divide the salad among individual salad plates and divide the reserved tempeh mixture among them.

SERVES 4

Per serving: 344 calories, 28 g fat, 14 g protein, 16 g carbohydrates, 4 g fiber, 0 mg cholesterol, 398 mg sodium

Note: Poaching tempeh mellows its flavor. Place the tempeh in a saucepan, cover with water, and simmer for 10 minutes. Drain and pat dry before using.

**Variation:** Regular dairy mayonnaise may be used instead of the soy mayonnaise.

## Soy Mayonnaise

*Several brands of commercially produced soy mayonnaise are available, both in natural food stores and in larger supermarkets. Two widely available brands are Vegenaise and Nayonaise. For those who prefer to make vegan mayonnaise from scratch, here's a recipe for a homemade version.*

1 cup soft regular or silken tofu

2 tablespoons fresh lemon juice

½ teaspoon salt

¼ teaspoon prepared yellow mustard

2 tablespoons canola oil

In a blender or food processor, blend the tofu, lemon juice, salt, and mustard until smooth. With the machine running, slowly add the oil until it is incorporated. Taste to adjust the seasoning. Transfer to a container with a tight-fitting lid and refrigerate until ready to use. Properly stored, the mayonnaise will keep for several days in the refrigerator.

MAKES ABOUT 1 CUP

Per 1 tablespoon: 25 calories, 2 g fat, 1 g protein, 0 g carbohydrates, 0 g fiber, 0 mg cholesterol, 75 mg sodium

# CRUNCHY VEGETABLE SLAW

*This vivacious slaw is a great way to use up those broccoli stems that we hate to throw away. Just peel them and run them through the shredding disk of your food processor.*

2 cups shredded, peeled broccoli stems

2 cups shredded red cabbage

1 yellow bell pepper, cut into thin slivers

2 tablespoons finely chopped fresh flat-leaf parsley

¼ cup extra virgin olive oil

2 tablespoons fresh lemon juice

¼ teaspoon celery salt

Freshly ground black pepper

In a large bowl, toss together the broccoli, cabbage, bell pepper, and parsley. Set aside. In a small bowl, combine the oil, lemon juice, celery salt, and pepper to taste. Blend well. Pour the dressing over the vegetables and toss to combine. Taste to adjust the seasoning. Cover and refrigerate until ready to serve.

**SERVES 4**

Per serving: 169 calories, 14 g fat, 3 g protein, 9 g carbohydrates, 4 g fiber, 0 mg cholesterol, 123 mg sodium

# SESAME COLESLAW WITH DAIKON, SNOW PEAS, AND GINGER

*Asian flavors dominate this crunchy coleslaw made with napa cabbage. A small amount of natural sweetener adds a nice flavor.*

2 tablespoons toasted sesame oil

2 teaspoons rice vinegar

1 teaspoon finely chopped fresh ginger

1 teaspoon fresh lime juice

1 teaspoon low-sodium tamari soy sauce

½ teaspoon agave syrup or a pinch of stevia (optional)

Salt and freshly ground black pepper

3 cups shredded napa cabbage

1 cup grated daikon radish

12 snow peas, cut diagonally into matchsticks

2 scallions, finely chopped

¼ cup grated carrot

2 tablespoons chopped fresh cilantro

2 tablespoons toasted sesame seeds

In a small bowl, combine the oil, vinegar, ginger, lime juice, tamari, agave syrup or stevia, and salt and pepper to taste. Stir well to blend and set aside. In a large bowl, combine the cabbage, daikon, snow peas, scallions, carrot, and cilantro. Pour the dressing over the vegetables and toss gently to coat. Taste to adjust the seasoning. Sprinkle with the sesame seeds. Refrigerate, covered, until ready to serve.

**SERVES 4**

Per serving: 119 calories, 9 g fat, 2 g protein, 7 g carbohydrates, 2 g fiber, 0 mg cholesterol, 97 mg sodium

## SOY-GOOD "EGG" SALAD

*Capers are listed as optional since they're not in everyone's pantry, but I highly recommend them for an added touch of piquancy. This cholesterol-free "egg salad" made with heart-healthy soy can be enjoyed on a bed of lettuce, stuffed inside a tomato, or as a low-carb sandwich filling on whole grain or sprouted bread. Soy mayonnaise is available in natural food stores and well-stocked supermarkets.*

⅓ cup soy mayonnaise

2 tablespoons tahini paste

1 tablespoon Dijon mustard

1 tablespoon fresh lemon juice

1 tablespoon white wine vinegar

½ teaspoon salt

¼ teaspoon ground paprika

⅛ teaspoon ground turmeric

⅛ teaspoon ground red pepper

1 pound extra-firm tofu, well drained, squeezed, and patted dry

⅓ cup finely chopped celery

¼ cup finely chopped fresh flat-leaf parsley

2 tablespoons chopped scallion

1 teaspoon capers, rinsed, drained, and chopped (optional)

In a small bowl, combine the mayonnaise, tahini, mustard, lemon juice, vinegar, salt, paprika, turmeric, and ground red pepper; blend well.

Place the tofu in a large bowl and crumble it with a fork. Add the celery, parsley, scallion, and capers. Stir in the mayonnaise mixture and blend well. Refrigerate for at least 30 minutes or overnight. When ready to serve, taste to adjust the seasoning.

**SERVES 4**

Per serving: 193 calories, 16 g fat, 9 g protein, 7 g carbohydrates, 2 g fiber, 0 mg cholesterol, 566 mg sodium

**Variation:** Regular mayonnaise may be used instead of soy mayonnaise.

## SOY: A TWO-FOR-ONE BONUS

Cholesterol watchers, take note: When you enjoy a soy-based meal such as "egg" salad made with tofu and soy mayo, you get a double bonus in the fight against high cholesterol. Studies show that soy helps reduce "bad" cholesterol. In addition, by choosing cholesterol-free soy foods instead of animal products, you avoid ingesting more cholesterol.

# MOROCCAN GREEN PEPPER SALAD

*Now that red and yellow bell peppers are on the culinary scene, green peppers are often passed over in favor of their sweeter counterparts, but this flavorful salad proves that green bells can still get rave reviews.*

3 green bell peppers

2 cucumbers, peeled, seeded, and cut into ½" dice

1 tomato, cut into ½" dice

¼ cup chopped fresh cilantro

2 tablespoons finely chopped onion

1 clove garlic, finely chopped

2 tablespoons extra virgin olive oil

1 tablespoon fresh lemon juice

½ teaspoon grated fresh ginger

½ teaspoon ground cumin

Salt and freshly ground black pepper

Roast the peppers over a gas flame, on a grill, or under a broiler until they are blackened all over. Place the blackened peppers inside a paper or plastic bag for 10 minutes to steam the skin loose, then scrape off the charred skin and remove the stems and seeds. Cut the peppers into ½" and place in a large bowl.

Add the cucumbers, tomato, cilantro, onion, garlic, oil, lemon juice, ginger, cumin, and salt and pepper to taste. Toss gently to combine. Serve at room temperature.

**SERVES 4**

Per serving: 114 calories, 7 g fat, 2 g protein, 11 g carbohydrates, 3 g fiber, 0 mg cholesterol, 7 mg sodium

## GREEN GOODNESS SALAD

*This "green on green" salad is especially delicious dressed with the equally verdant Goddess-Inspired Dressing.*

4 ounces green beans, steamed and cut into 1" pieces

2 ounces snow peas, blanched and cut into 1" pieces

1 cucumber, peeled, quartered lengthwise, seeded, and thinly sliced

1 rib celery, thinly sliced

3 cups torn romaine lettuce

2 cups coarsely chopped watercress (large stems removed)

¼ cup walnut pieces, lightly toasted

Goddess-Inspired Dressing (page 173)

In a large bowl, combine the beans, snow peas, cucumber, celery, lettuce, watercress, and walnuts. Toss gently to combine. When ready to serve, toss the salad with the dressing or serve the dressing on the side.

### SERVES 4

Per serving: 74 calories, 4 g fat, 3 g protein, 7 g carbohydrates, 4 g fiber, 0 mg cholesterol, 25 mg sodium

## FOOD FOR THOUGHT

A high-fiber, whole foods, plant-based diet can provide the greatest possible benefits for disease risk reduction, weight loss, and general well-being. As a bonus, by doing this, we help to protect the environment and promote compassion for all living things.

# RAGIN' CAJUN TASTES-LIKE-CHICKEN SALAD

*Try this spicy, hearty salad on a bed of salad greens, on whole grain or low-carb bread, or rolled up in a lettuce leaf for a satisfying lunch. Instead of tempeh, try this recipe with chopped chicken-style seitan or other similar meat alternative, available in natural food stores and larger supermarkets. The optional jalapeño will add heat, but if you prefer more flavor without the heat, consider using mild canned chiles instead.*

⅓ cup soy mayonnaise

1 teaspoon Dijon mustard

1 teaspoon fresh lemon juice

¼ teaspoon ground cumin

1 package (8 ounces) tempeh, poached and finely chopped (see note)

½ cup chickpeas, coarsely chopped

½ cup finely chopped celery

¼ cup finely chopped green bell pepper

2 tablespoons chopped scallion

1 tablespoon finely chopped fresh flat-leaf parsley

1 teaspoon finely chopped canned jalapeño chile pepper (optional)

2 tablespoons chopped pimiento-stuffed green olives

Salt and freshly ground black pepper

Tabasco

In a large bowl, whisk together the mayonnaise, mustard, lemon juice, and cumin. Add the tempeh, chickpeas, celery, bell pepper, scallion, parsley, jalapeño, olives, salt and pepper to taste, and Tabasco to taste. Mix until well combined. Cover and refrigerate for 30 minutes to an hour to allow the flavors to develop.

**SERVES 4**

Per serving: 203 calories, 10 g fat, 14 g protein, 15 g carbohydrates, 5 g fiber, 0 mg cholesterol, 341 mg sodium

Note: Poaching tempeh mellows its flavor. Place the tempeh in a saucepan, cover with water, and simmer for 10 minutes. Drain and pat dry before using.

**Variation:** Regular mayonnaise may be used instead of soy mayo.

# EDAMAME, SNOW PEAS, AND BEAN SPROUTS WITH GINGER-LIME VINAIGRETTE

*Protein-rich edamame (green soybeans) were once found only in specialty stores, but now they're available both fresh and frozen in most larger supermarkets. For convenience, buy edamame that have already been shelled. This flavorful Asian-style salad can be served either chilled or at room temperature.*

3 tablespoons fresh lime juice

1 teaspoon grated fresh ginger

1 clove garlic, chopped

2 teaspoons finely chopped fresh flat-leaf parsley or cilantro

1 scallion, finely chopped

½ teaspoon salt

⅛ teaspoon ground red pepper

2 tablespoons toasted sesame oil

2 tablespoons canola oil

3 cups bean sprouts, blanched

4 ounces snow peas, blanched

1 cup fresh or frozen shelled edamame, cooked

In a small bowl, combine the lime juice, ginger, garlic, parsley or cilantro, scallion, salt, ground red pepper, sesame oil, and canola oil. Mix well. Set aside.

Make sure the bean sprouts, snow peas, and edamame are well drained and blotted free of any excess liquid, then combine them in a large bowl. Pour on the reserved dressing and toss to combine.

**SERVES 4**

Per serving: 261 calories, 18 g fat, 12 g protein, 16 g carbohydrates, 5 g fiber, 0 mg cholesterol, 309 mg sodium

# FENNEL SALAD WITH SUN-DRIED TOMATOES, BLACK OLIVES, AND PINE NUTS

*The intense flavors of the kalamata olives and sun-dried tomatoes combine with the crunchy texture of fennel and pine nuts for a flavorful and satisfying salad.*

1 large fennel bulb, quartered lengthwise and thinly sliced

1 red bell pepper, finely chopped

¼ cup chopped kalamata olives

¼ cup chopped fresh flat-leaf parsley

2 tablespoons sun-dried tomatoes, soaked and chopped

1 tablespoon chopped scallion

3 tablespoons olive oil

2 teaspoons fresh lemon juice

Salt and freshly ground black pepper

Torn mixed salad greens

2 tablespoons pine nuts, toasted

In a large bowl, combine the fennel, bell pepper, olives, parsley, tomatoes, scallion, oil, lemon juice, and salt and pepper to taste. Set aside. When ready to serve, line individual salad plates with the salad greens, spoon the reserved mixture onto the greens, and sprinkle with the pine nuts.

**SERVES 4**

Per serving: 167 calories, 14 g fat, 2 g protein, 9 g carbohydrates, 3 g fiber, 0 mg cholesterol, 191 mg sodium

# AVOCADO-TOPPED GAZPACHO SALAD

*This crisp and crunchy salad topped with buttery avocado is a filling and attractive way to enjoy the flavors of gazpacho soup in a salad. Best of all, almost all of it can be made ahead.*

1 red bell pepper, finely chopped

1 cucumber, peeled, seeded, and finely chopped

1 tomato, seeded and finely chopped

2 scallions, finely chopped

1 garlic clove, finely chopped

1 teaspoon finely chopped canned jalapeño chile pepper

2 tablespoons olive oil

1 tablespoon fresh lime juice

1 tablespoon finely chopped fresh flat-leaf parsley

Salt and freshly ground black pepper

5 cups torn mixed salad greens

1 small ripe avocado

In a large bowl, combine the bell pepper, cucumber, tomato, scallions, garlic, jalapeño, oil, lime juice, parsley, and salt and pepper to taste. Cover and set aside for 30 minutes or refrigerate overnight. Divide the salad greens among individual salad plates and top with the reserved gazpacho mixture. Halve and pit the avocado and cut it into ½" dice. Divide the avocado among the salads and serve at once.

**SERVES 4**

Per serving: 154 calories, 12 g fat, 3 g protein, 12 g carbohydrates, 6 g fiber, 0 mg cholesterol, 16 mg sodium

# CHICORY AND BUTTERHEAD LETTUCE SALAD WITH MUSHROOMS, RED PEPPERS, AND ALMONDS

*Chicory, or curly endive, is a crisp, bitter green that contrasts with sweet, mild butterhead lettuce. Here, it's further augmented by a tasty trio of mushrooms, almonds, and red bell peppers. If butterhead lettuce is unavailable, use Boston lettuce or another tender, soft leaf lettuce.*

3 tablespoons white wine vinegar

1 teaspoon finely chopped garlic

Pinch of stevia

¼ teaspoon salt

⅛ teaspoon ground red pepper

⅛ teaspoon mustard powder

⅓ cup olive oil

1 small head chicory, coarsely chopped

1 small head butterhead lettuce, torn into bite-size pieces

1 cup sliced white mushrooms

½ cup chopped red bell pepper

½ cup slivered almonds, toasted

1 tablespoon finely chopped fresh flat-leaf parsley

In a small bowl, combine the vinegar, garlic, stevia, salt, ground red pepper, and mustard; mix well. Blend in the oil and set aside. In a large bowl, combine the chicory, lettuce, mushrooms, bell pepper, almonds, and parsley. Pour the dressing over the salad and toss lightly to coat.

## SERVES 4

Per serving: 248 calories, 24 g fat, 4 g protein, 6 g carbohydrates, 2 g fiber, 0 mg cholesterol, 147 mg sodium

# RADICCHIO AND BABY SPINACH SALAD WITH WALNUT-CUCUMBER DRESSING

*Walnut oil is quite expensive, so if you'd like to make a more economical version of this salad, substitute olive oil for the walnut oil.*

1 cucumber, peeled, seeded, and coarsely chopped

1 large shallot, chopped

2 tablespoons walnut oil

¼ cup tarragon vinegar, sherry vinegar, or white wine vinegar

¾ teaspoon salt

4 cups baby spinach

1 head radicchio, halved lengthwise and cut crosswise into thin strips

½ cucumber, peeled, halved lengthwise, seeded, and cut crosswise into paper-thin slices

⅓ cup walnut pieces, toasted

Freshly ground black pepper

In a food processor or blender, blend the chopped cucumber, shallot, oil, vinegar, and salt until smooth. Set aside. In a large bowl, combine the spinach and radicchio. Add the dressing and toss to combine. Divide the salad among individual salad plates and garnish with the cucumber slices, walnuts, and a few grinds of black pepper.

## SERVES 4

Per serving: 189 calories, 17 g fat, 4 g protein, 8 g carbohydrates, 3 g fiber, 0 mg cholesterol, 517 mg sodium

# WINTER GREENS AND FENNEL WITH PECANS AND DIJON-MISO DRESSING

*The distinctive flavors of fennel, watercress, and chicory are complemented by a zesty mustard-miso dressing and accented with pecans. Try different greens such as chard, spinach, or romaine lettuce instead of the chicory, watercress, or even the fennel.*

1 clove garlic, crushed

2 tablespoons red wine vinegar

1 tablespoon white miso paste

1 tablespoon finely chopped fresh flat-leaf parsley

1 teaspoon Dijon mustard

1 teaspoon finely chopped chives

¼ cup olive oil

Salt and freshly ground black pepper

1 bunch watercress, stemmed and chopped

1 head chicory (curly endive), torn into small pieces

1 large fennel bulb, quartered and thinly sliced

¼ cup pecan pieces, toasted

In a small bowl, combine the garlic, vinegar, miso, parsley, mustard, chives, oil, and salt and pepper to taste. Whisk the dressing until it is emulsified. Set aside to allow its flavors to blend. In a large bowl, combine the watercress, chicory, and fennel. To serve, toss the salad with the reserved dressing and sprinkle with the pecans.

## SERVES 4

Per serving: 206 calories, 19 g fat, 3 g protein, 8 g carbohydrates, 3 g fiber, 0 mg cholesterol, 192 mg sodium

## FOUR-OF-HEARTS SALAD

*Isn't it romantic? This delicious salad made with romaine hearts, artichoke hearts, hearts of palm, and celery hearts is also very elegant. Serve it as the first course to a special meal. The radish slices add a nice pink blush to the salad, but a garnish of edible flower petals would be absolutely sublime.*

2 romaine lettuce hearts

1 package (9 ounces) frozen artichoke hearts, cooked and sliced

1 can (14 ounces) hearts of palm, drained and sliced

½ cup chopped celery hearts

2 red radishes, thinly sliced

3 tablespoons white wine vinegar

1 shallot, finely chopped

Salt and freshly ground black pepper

⅓ cup extra virgin olive oil

Tear the romaine into bite-size pieces and place in a large bowl. Add the artichoke hearts, hearts of palm, celery, and radishes. Set aside. In a small bowl, combine the vinegar, shallot, and salt and pepper to taste. Whisk in the olive oil and pour the dressing over the salad; toss gently to combine.

**SERVES 4**

Per serving: 220 calories, 19 g fat, 5 g protein, 12 g carbohydrates, 7 g fiber, 0 mg cholesterol, 411 mg sodium

# GRILLED RADICCHIO ON SHAVED FENNEL

*Both fennel and radicchio are delicious served raw or grilled. Here's a salad that incorporates raw fennel with grilled radicchio—my favorite combination because grilling gives a hearty, robust quality to the radicchio, and keeping the fennel raw retains more of its licorice flavor. See if you don't agree.*

> 2 small heads radicchio, halved
>
> Olive oil
>
> 2 large fennel bulbs, halved lengthwise
>
> ½ cup pecan halves, toasted
>
> ¼ cup white wine vinegar
>
> 1 teaspoon Dijon mustard
>
> ½ teaspoon salt
>
> ¼ teaspoon freshly ground black pepper

Heat the grill. Coat the radicchio with olive oil and place on the grill. Watching carefully to be sure it does not burn, turn frequently and brush with more oil, if necessary. Grill until soft and the outer leaves are browned, about 10 minutes total. Set aside.

Cut the fennel crosswise into paper-thin slices and place in a large bowl. Add the pecans. In a small bowl, combine the vinegar, mustard, salt, and pepper. Whisk in ¼ cup olive oil to blend and pour the dressing onto the fennel and pecans. Toss gently to coat. Divide the salad among individual salad plates and top with the grilled radicchio.

### SERVES 4

Per serving: 272 calories, 25 g fat, 3 g protein, 13 g carbohydrates, 5 g fiber, 0 mg cholesterol, 390 mg sodium

# JAPANESE EGGPLANT–WALNUT SALAD

*This salad is a symphony of flavors and textures, as meaty eggplant flavored with a walnut oil, sherry, and ginger marinade is nestled on a bed of crisp romaine and topped with crunchy pieces of toasted walnuts. The optional red bell pepper and daikon add additional color and textural contrast.*

3 Japanese eggplants, halved lengthwise

2 tablespoons canola oil

2 tablespoons toasted walnut or sesame oil

2 tablespoons rice vinegar

1 tablespoon low-sodium tamari soy sauce

1 tablespoon dry sherry

½ teaspoon agave syrup

1 teaspoon finely chopped garlic

1 teaspoon grated fresh ginger

¼ teaspoon red-pepper flakes

1 head romaine lettuce, cut crosswise into thin strips

½ cup walnut pieces, toasted

½ red bell pepper, cut into thin matchsticks (optional)

1 piece (2 inches) daikon radish, cut into thin matchsticks (optional)

Preheat the oven to 375°F. Place the eggplants in a lightly oiled baking pan, cut side down. Bake until tender, about 30 minutes. Cool slightly, then peel the eggplants and cut into 1" cubes. Place in a shallow bowl and set aside.

In a small bowl, combine the canola oil, walnut or sesame oil, vinegar, tamari, sherry, agave syrup, garlic, ginger, and red-pepper flakes. Mix well and pour over the eggplant. Cover and refrigerate for 1 hour.

Divide the lettuce among individual salad plates. Spoon the eggplant mixture on top of the lettuce and sprinkle with the walnuts, bell pepper (if using), and daikon (if using). Drizzle any remaining dressing over the salad.

**SERVES 4**

Per serving: 295 calories, 24 g fat, 6 g protein, 18 g carbohydrates, 8 g fiber, 0 mg cholesterol, 163 mg sodium

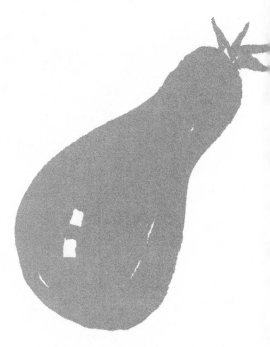

# TABBOULEH-STYLE QUINOA SALAD

*Inspired by the traditional salad made with bulgur, this lighter variation is made with quinoa, a small, protein-rich grain. The recipe testers agreed that this was the best tabbouleh they ever tasted.*

2 cups water

Salt

1 cup quinoa, rinsed well and drained

1 cucumber, peeled, seeded, and chopped

1 tomato, chopped

½ cup cooked chickpeas

2 scallions, finely chopped

½ cup finely chopped fresh flat-leaf parsley

⅓ cup olive oil

3 tablespoons fresh lemon juice

4 cups shredded mixed salad greens

Bring the water to a boil in a medium saucepan and add salt to taste. Stir in the quinoa and reduce the heat to low. Cover and simmer until the water is absorbed, about 15 minutes. Drain and blot the quinoa with paper towels to remove any excess moisture.

In a large bowl, mix together the quinoa, cucumber, tomato, chickpeas, scallions, and parsley. In a small bowl, combine the oil, lemon juice, and salt to taste. Pour the dressing over the quinoa mixture and mix gently to combine. Cover and refrigerate for at least 1 hour. Serve the quinoa over the mixed greens.

**SERVES 6**

Per serving: 254 calories, 13 g fat, 6 g protein, 28 g carbohydrates, 4 g fiber, 0 mg cholesterol, 74 mg sodium

## QUICK QUINOA QUIZ

Did you know that quinoa is an ancient grain of the Incas? Its name means "the mother grain." Because it contains all the essential amino acids, it is considered a complete protein and is lower in carbohydrates than other grains. Dubbed "the supergrain of the future," quinoa is also rich in B vitamins, iron, calcium, and vitamin E. Quinoa has a distinctive, nutty flavor and a light, fluffy texture.

# CHAPTER FIVE

# MORE THAN SIDES

What many people consider side dishes are often much more than that to a vegetarian. In this chapter, for example, Edamame and Yellow Pepper Succotash and Garlicky Escarole and White Beans are rich enough in protein, vitamins, and minerals that they can be enjoyed as main courses as well as side dishes. Add strips of tofu or a vegetarian meat alternative to Sesame Vegetable Stir-Fry or Szechuan Portobello Mushrooms and String Beans and you have complete, well-balanced meals. On the other hand, some recipes are at their best when playing a supporting role. For example, Cauliflower "Mashed Potatoes," a popular low-carb alternative to the starchy tuber, are especially tasty when topped with your favorite roasted vegetables or seared portobello mushroom strips and a rich brown gravy.

# SIMMERED ZUCCHINI WITH ONION AND TOMATOES

*My mother prepared zucchini this way when I was a child, and I'm still making it the same way today. To turn this from a side dish into a main dish, divide two or three thawed veggie burgers into quarters, roll them into small balls, and brown them in a skillet—or buy some ready-made veggie "meatballs"—and add them to the zucchini at serving time.*

   1 tablespoon olive oil
   ¼ cup chopped sweet yellow onion
   4 zucchini, cut into ¼" slices
   1 can (14½ ounces) finely diced tomatoes, drained
   Salt and freshly ground black pepper
   2 tablespoons chopped fresh flat-leaf parsley
   1 tablespoon chopped fresh basil

Heat the oil in a large skillet or saucepan over medium heat. Add the onion, cover, and cook for 2 minutes, until softened. Add the zucchini, cover, and cook for 5 minutes longer, stirring occasionally, to soften. Stir in the tomatoes and salt and pepper to taste. Cover and cook until the vegetables are tender and the flavors have had time to mingle, 10 to 15 minutes. Stir in the parsley and basil. Serve hot.

**SERVES 4**

Per serving: 75 calories, 4 g fat, 2 g protein, 10 g carbohydrates, 3 g fiber, 0 mg cholesterol, 136 mg sodium

# SZECHUAN PORTOBELLO MUSHROOMS AND STRING BEANS

*Portobello mushrooms lend their meaty texture to this flavorful stir-fry made with fresh green beans and fragrant Asian seasonings, including ginger and toasted sesame oil. Szechuan food is typically spicy hot, but if you prefer to cut back on the red-pepper flakes, there's enough flavor in this dish without them. To turn this into a main course, stir-fry strips of extra-firm tofu.*

8 ounces green beans, cut in half

1 tablespoon canola oil

4 large portobello mushroom caps, gills removed and caps cut into ¼" strips

2 cloves garlic, finely chopped

2 teaspoons finely chopped fresh ginger

2 tablespoons chopped scallion

2 tablespoons low-sodium tamari soy sauce

1 tablespoon mirin

½ teaspoon red-pepper flakes, or to taste

1 tablespoon toasted sesame oil

Lightly steam the beans until just tender, about 5 minutes. Rinse under cold water to stop the cooking process. Drain, pat dry, and set aside.

Heat the canola oil in a large skillet over medium-high heat. Add the mushrooms, garlic, ginger, and scallion and stir-fry until the mushrooms soften, about 5 minutes. Add the tamari, mirin, red-pepper flakes, and reserved beans. Stir-fry until hot and well combined, about 2 minutes longer. Drizzle with the sesame oil and serve hot.

**SERVES 4**

Per serving: 101 calories, 7 g fat, 2 g protein, 7 g carbohydrates, 2 g fiber, 0 mg cholesterol, 304 mg sodium

# EDAMAME AND YELLOW PEPPER SUCCOTASH

*Regular succotash made with lima beans and corn averages about 22 grams of carbs per ½ cup. And what succotash lover can eat just ½ cup? Try this retooled lower-carb interpretation made with protein-rich edamame instead of limas and a fine dice of sweet yellow pepper and yellow summer squash to replace the high-glycemic corn.*

1 tablespoon olive oil

1 yellow bell pepper, cut into ¼" dice

1 yellow summer squash, cut into ¼" dice

Salt and freshly ground black pepper

2 cups fresh or frozen shelled edamame, cooked

1 tablespoon chopped fresh flat-leaf parsley

Heat the oil in a large saucepan over medium heat. Add the bell pepper, cover, and cook for 5 minutes to soften. Add the squash and salt and pepper to taste. Cover and cook until the vegetables are tender, about 5 minutes. Stir in the edamame and continue to cook until heated through. Taste to adjust the seasoning. Sprinkle with the parsley and serve hot.

**SERVES 4**

Per serving: 223 calories, 12 g fat, 17 g protein, 17 g carbohydrates, 6 g fiber, 0 mg cholesterol, 21 mg sodium

# SESAME VEGETABLE STIR-FRY

*As a side dish, this vegetable mélange couldn't be prettier or more flavorful. It transforms easily into a hearty main dish if you add diced tofu or seitan to the stir-fry and serve it over brown rice or quinoa.*

2 teaspoons canola oil

1 tablespoon finely chopped fresh ginger

1 red bell pepper, cut into thin strips

2 scallions, finely chopped

1 head broccoli, cut into small florets and blanched

8 ounces white mushrooms, sliced

1 bunch watercress, stemmed and coarsely chopped

¼ cup canned sliced water chestnuts

2 tablespoons low-sodium tamari soy sauce

2 teaspoons toasted sesame oil

1 tablespoon toasted sesame seeds

Heat the canola oil in a large skillet or wok over medium-high heat. Add the ginger and cook until fragrant, about 30 seconds. Add the bell pepper, scallions, broccoli, mushrooms, watercress, water chestnuts, and tamari. Stir-fry until the vegetables are softened but not overcooked, about 4 to 5 minutes. Serve drizzled with the sesame oil and sprinkled with the sesame seeds.

**SERVES 4**

Per serving: 121 calories, 6 g fat, 6 g protein, 12 g carbohydrates, 5 g fiber, 0 mg cholesterol, 339 mg sodium

# GARLICKY ESCAROLE AND WHITE BEANS

*This classic Tuscan dish is ideal for low-carb vegetarian dining. Escarole is rich in iron and vitamins, and the beans provide protein and fiber, as well as "good" carbs.*

1 large head escarole, coarsely chopped
1 tablespoon olive oil
2–3 cloves garlic, finely chopped
1½ cups cooked white beans
¼ teaspoon red-pepper flakes (optional)
Salt and freshly ground black pepper

Cook the escarole in a pot of boiling salted water until wilted, about 3 minutes. Drain well and set aside.

Heat the oil in a large skillet over medium heat. Add the garlic and cook until fragrant, about 30 seconds. Add the reserved escarole and cook until tender, stirring occasionally, about 5 minutes. Add the beans, red-pepper flakes, and salt and pepper to taste. Cook for 10 minutes longer on low heat, stirring, to heat through and blend flavors.

**SERVES 4**

Per serving: 114 calories, 4 g fat, 7 g protein, 19 g carbohydrates, 9 g fiber, 0 mg cholesterol, 28 mg sodium

# BRAISED BOK CHOY WITH WALNUTS AND GINGER

*Baby bok choy are more tender than the large ones, and they make a lovely presentation. But you can also use the large kind, cut into small pieces. The flavors will remain the same.*

- 1 tablespoon canola oil
- 1 teaspoon finely chopped fresh ginger
- 1 teaspoon finely chopped garlic
- 4 heads baby bok choy, halved lengthwise
- 2 tablespoons chopped scallion
- 2 tablespoons low-sodium tamari soy sauce
- 1 tablespoon sake or mirin
- 1 tablespoon water
- ¼ cup walnut pieces, toasted

Heat the oil in a wok or large skillet over medium-high heat. Add the ginger and garlic; stir-fry until fragrant, about 30 seconds. Add the bok choy, scallion, tamari, sake or mirin, and water; stir-fry to coat. Reduce the heat to low, cover, and simmer until the vegetables are tender, 12 to 15 minutes. When ready to serve, add the walnuts and toss gently to coat. Serve hot.

## SERVES 4

Per serving: 200 calories, 10 g fat, 14 g protein, 21 g carbohydrates, 9 g fiber, 0 mg cholesterol, 547 mg sodium

# BROCCOLI RABE WITH GARLIC AND PINE NUTS

*Also known as rapini, broccoli rabe is an Italian vegetable that is winning admirers in this country. A favorite way to prepare it is with garlic and olive oil. Pine nuts are added here for protein, crunch, and flavor.*

1 pound broccoli rabe (rapini)
1 tablespoon olive oil
2 cloves garlic, crushed
Salt and freshly ground black pepper
¼ cup pine nuts, toasted

Trim the tough ends from the stalks and coarsely chop the broccoli rabe. Cook in a pot of boiling salted water until tender, 5 to 7 minutes. Drain and pat dry.

Heat the oil in a large skillet over medium heat. Add the garlic, then add the broccoli rabe and salt and pepper to taste. Cook, stirring, until hot, about 5 minutes. Serve sprinkled with the pine nuts.

**SERVES 4**

Per serving: 100 calories, 8 g fat, 5 g protein, 6 g carbohydrates, 0 g fiber, 0 mg cholesterol, 21 mg sodium

# INDIAN-STYLE SPINACH WITH MUSHROOMS AND TOMATO

*Whether raw or cooked, steamed, creamed, or stir-fried, spinach is enjoyed the world over for its great taste and iron-rich nutrition. This Indian-style preparation of spinach and mushrooms is one you'll want to add to your repertoire—it's quick and easy to make as well as bursting with flavor.*

1 pound fresh spinach

2 teaspoons canola oil

8 ounces white mushrooms, sliced

1 teaspoon grated fresh ginger

¼ teaspoon ground cumin

¼ teaspoon red-pepper flakes

1 cup finely chopped tomatoes

Salt

Steam the spinach until tender, about 3 minutes. Drain well and place in a blender or food processor; puree. Set aside.

Heat the oil in a large skillet over medium heat. Add the mushrooms, ginger, cumin, and red-pepper flakes; cook, stirring, for 1 minute. Stir in the tomatoes and salt to taste. Cook for 3 minutes, then stir in the reserved spinach and continue cooking until the mixture is hot and well blended.

**SERVES 4**

Per serving: 57 calories, 3 g fat, 4 g protein, 6 g carbohydrates, 3 g fiber, 0 mg cholesterol, 151 mg sodium

# ROASTED ASPARAGUS WITH HEART-HEALTHY HOLLANDAISE

*Roasting asparagus at high heat brings out its flavor. Irresistible in its own right, it's elevated to supreme dining pleasure when you serve it with this egg-free hollandaise alternative.*

1½ pounds asparagus spears
1 tablespoon olive oil
Salt and freshly ground black pepper
Heart-Healthy Hollandaise (page 172)

Preheat the oven to 450°F. Place the asparagus on a lightly oiled baking sheet in a single layer. Drizzle with the oil and salt and pepper to taste. Roast the asparagus until just tender, 7 to 10 minutes, depending on the thickness of the spears. Serve hot with the hollandaise.

**SERVES 4**

Per serving: 56 calories, 1 g fat, 4 g protein, 7 g carbohydrates, 4 g fiber, 0 mg cholesterol, 0 mg sodium

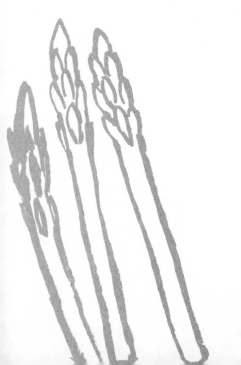

# PROVENÇALE GREEN BEANS AND MUSHROOMS

*The inclusion of tomatoes, garlic, and olive oil is often indicative of a recipe from the French region of Provence, famous for its delicious vegetable mélanges like this one made with green beans and mushrooms.*

    1 pound green beans
    1 tablespoon olive oil
    2 shallots, finely chopped
    2 cloves garlic, finely chopped
    8 ounces white mushrooms, sliced
    1½ cups finely diced fresh or canned tomatoes
    Salt and freshly ground black pepper

Lightly steam the beans until just tender. Run cold water over the beans to stop the cooking process. Drain and set aside.

Heat the oil in a large skillet over medium heat. Add the shallots and garlic, cover, and cook until softened, about 2 minutes. Add the mushrooms and cook until they begin to soften, 3 to 5 minutes. Stir in the tomatoes, reserved beans, and salt and pepper to taste. Simmer, stirring occasionally, until the vegetables are hot and the flavors are well combined, about 10 minutes.

**SERVES 4**

Per serving: 96 calories, 4 g fat, 4 g protein, 13 g carbohydrates, 6 g fiber, 0 mg cholesterol, 6 mg sodium

# SAUTÉED CUCUMBERS AND WATERCRESS

*Usually enjoyed raw in salads, cucumbers and watercress are surprisingly tasty when sautéed in olive oil.*

2 large cucumbers, peeled, halved lengthwise, and seeded
1 teaspoon salt
1 tablespoon olive oil
1 bunch watercress, stemmed and coarsely chopped
Freshly ground black pepper

Cut the cucumbers into ¼" slices and toss with the salt in a colander. Let drain for 15 minutes. Rinse under cold running water and drain again. Pat dry and set aside.

Heat the oil in a large skillet over medium-high heat. Add the cucumber slices and cook until crisp-tender, about 5 minutes. Reduce the heat to low, stir in the watercress, and cook until wilted, about 3 minutes. Season with pepper to taste.

**SERVES 4**

Per serving: 49 calories, 4 g fat, 1 g protein, 4 g carbohydrates, 1 g fiber, 0 mg cholesterol, 106 mg sodium

# BRAISED FENNEL AND BABY ARTICHOKES

*Serve this delicious dish garnished with not only lemon wedges but also chopped fennel fronds, chopped dill, and a drizzle of olive oil, if desired.*

- 1 tablespoon olive oil
- 2 small fennel bulbs, quartered
- 3 baby artichokes, halved
- ¼ cup water
- 2 tablespoons white wine
- 1 tablespoon fresh lemon juice
- Salt and freshly ground black pepper
- Lemon wedges

Heat the oil in a saucepan or deep skillet over medium heat. Add the fennel and artichokes and cook until lightly browned and slightly softened, about 5 minutes. Add the water, wine, lemon juice, and salt and pepper to taste. Reduce the heat to low, cover, and cook until the vegetables are tender, about 20 minutes. Serve with lemon wedges.

**SERVES 4**

Per serving: 87 calories, 4 g fat, 3 g protein, 12 g carbohydrates, 5 g fiber, 0 mg cholesterol, 91 mg sodium

# GREEN BEAN CASSEROLE REDUX

*If that same old green bean casserole keeps turning up on your holiday table, maybe it's time to try a healthier, updated version and start a new tradition.*

1 tablespoon olive oil

½ cup chopped onion

3 cups chopped white mushrooms

2 cloves garlic, chopped

1 cup cooked white beans

1 cup soy sour cream

1 cup soy milk

Salt and freshly ground black pepper

1½ pounds green beans, cut into 1" pieces and blanched

⅓ cup chopped walnuts

Preheat the oven to 350°F.

Heat the oil in a large skillet over medium-high heat. Add the onion, cover, and cook until softened, about 3 minutes. Add the mushrooms and garlic and stir until softened, about 3 minutes. Scoop out about 1 cup of the mushrooms and set aside.

Place the white beans in a blender. Add the remaining onion and mushroom mixture, sour cream, milk, and salt and pepper to taste. Blend until smooth.

Place the green beans in a 2-quart casserole. Stir in the sauce and the reserved mushrooms. Cover and bake for 50 minutes, until the green beans are nearly tender. Uncover and sprinkle with the walnuts. Bake uncovered until the beans are tender and the walnuts are toasted, about 10 minutes.

**SERVES 6**

Per serving: 245 calories, 16 g fat, 9 g protein, 21 g carbohydrates, 8 g fiber, 0 mg cholesterol, 28 g sodium

**Variation:** Dairy sour cream and cow's milk may be used to replace the soy products.

# CAULIFLOWER AND GREEN BEANS
# WITH MUSTARD–DILL SAUCE

*The creamy mustard dill sauce complements a variety of vegetables, but I think it is especially good over cauliflower and green beans.*

½ cup soft tofu, well drained

2 tablespoons coarse-grained mustard

1 tablespoon Dijon mustard

1 teaspoon fresh lemon juice

3 tablespoons finely chopped fresh dill or 1 tablespoon dried dillweed

½ teaspoon salt

⅛ teaspoon freshly ground black pepper

1 pound green beans

1 small head cauliflower, cut into florets

Use an immersion blender or small food processor to blend the tofu, coarse mustard, Dijon mustard, lemon juice, dill, salt, and pepper until smooth. Transfer to a small saucepan and heat over low heat until warm. Taste to adjust the seasoning. Keep the sauce warm over very low heat while you cook the vegetables or reheat it when ready to serve.

Steam the beans until tender, about 7 minutes. Steam the cauliflower until tender, about 5 minutes. To serve, arrange the vegetables decoratively on a platter and top with the sauce.

**SERVES 4**

Per serving: 84 calories, 2 g fat, 5 g protein, 12 g carbohydrates, 6 g fiber, 0 mg cholesterol, 597 mg sodium

**Variation:** Yogurt may be used to replace the tofu.

# CAULIFLOWER "MASHED POTATOES"

*Nothing's going to convince anyone these are real mashed potatoes, but they sure do look like the genuine article and happen to taste great topped with a rich brown gravy like Wild Mushroom Sauce on page 164. Garlic lovers can puree some roasted garlic along with the cauliflower for garlic mashed cauliflower.*

> 1 head cauliflower, coarsely chopped
> 1 teaspoon extra virgin olive oil or nonhydrogenated, trans-free margarine
> Salt and freshly ground black pepper

Steam the cauliflower until tender, about 10 minutes. In a food processor, blend the cauliflower, oil, and salt and pepper to taste until smooth. Transfer to a serving bowl and serve hot.

## SERVES 4

Per serving: 58 calories, 1 g fat, 4 g protein, 11 g carbohydrates, 5 g fiber, 0 mg cholesterol, 63 mg sodium

## FAT FACTS

• Incorporate cooking techniques that do not require added fat, such as steaming, broiling, grilling, or roasting.

• To cut down on fat, use a nonstick skillet or wok and a small amount of cooking spray or olive oil when sautéing or stir-frying.

• Braised vegetables require just 2 teaspoons of olive oil—or even just a coating of cooking spray—in a nonstick skillet before adding a few tablespoons of liquid. Then cover and cook over low heat.

# CHIPOTLE MASHED CAULIFLOWER

*The smoky heat of the pureed chipotle chile enlivens the mild flavor of the mashed cauliflower to entice the chile-heads at your table.*

> 1 head cauliflower, coarsely chopped
>
> 1 teaspoon chipotle chile pepper, canned in adobo sauce
>
> 1 tablespoon olive oil
>
> Salt

Steam the cauliflower until soft, about 10 minutes.

In a food processor, blend the chile pepper and oil until smooth. Add the cauliflower and salt to taste. Blend until smooth and well combined. Serve hot.

**SERVES 4**

Per serving: 83 calories, 4 g fat, 4 g protein, 11 g carbohydrates, 5 g fiber, 0 mg cholesterol, 64 mg sodium

# "BACONY" SIMMERED COLLARDS

*Collard greens, a perennial favorite of the South, are often cooked with a piece of salt pork or bacon for flavoring. In this recipe, the smoky flavor is amply provided by soy bacon bits.*

1½ pounds fresh collard greens
1 tablespoon olive oil
¼ cup finely chopped onion
1 clove garlic, finely chopped
¼ cup water
2–3 tablespoons soy bacon bits
Salt and freshly ground black pepper

Cook the collard greens in a pot of boiling salted water until tender, about 30 minutes. Drain well. Coarsely chop the greens, then set aside.

Heat the oil in a large skillet over medium heat. Add the onion and garlic, cover, and cook until softened, about 3 minutes. Add the reserved collards, water, bacon bits, and salt and pepper to taste. Simmer to heat through and combine the flavors, about 10 minutes. Serve hot.

**SERVES 4**

Per serving: 91 calories, 5 g fat, 5 g protein, 10 g carbohydrates, 5 g fiber, 0 mg cholesterol, 38 mg sodium

# GREEN BEAN BULGUR PILAF

*The green beans add a lovely accent of color and the slivered almonds provide light crunch in this fragrant, hearty dish made with bulgur, a quick-cooking grain also known as cracked wheat. The mint and almonds give the dish a Middle Eastern accent—for an Italian nuance, substitute basil and pine nuts.*

1 tablespoon olive oil

¼ cup finely chopped onion

1 cup medium bulgur

2 cups boiling water

8 ounces green beans, cut into ½" pieces

Salt and freshly ground black pepper

¼ cup slivered almonds, toasted

1 tablespoon chopped fresh mint

In a large skillet, heat the oil over medium heat. Add the onion, cover, and cook until softened. Add the bulgur and stir to combine. Stir in the water. Add the green beans, and season with salt and pepper to taste. Remove the skillet from the heat. Cover until the green beans are tender and the liquid has been absorbed, about 15 minutes. Stir in the almonds and mint.

**SERVES 6**

Per serving: 140 calories, 5 g fat, 4 g protein, 22 g carbohydrates, 6 g fiber, 0 mg cholesterol, 4 mg sodium

# RAID-THE-GARDEN RATATOUILLE

*The bane of this popular vegetable dish from Provence is that it is usually served with crusty French bread. Fortunately, ratatouille is also delicious without bread—proving that there can be life after baguettes.*

2 tablespoons olive oil

½ cup chopped onion

1 eggplant, cut into ½" cubes

1 red bell pepper, cut into ½" dice

2 cloves garlic, finely chopped

2 zucchini, halved lengthwise and cut into ½" slices

1 cup finely diced canned tomatoes, drained

1 teaspoon dried thyme

Salt and freshly ground black pepper

1 tablespoon chopped fresh flat-leaf parsley

1 tablespoon chopped fresh basil

Heat the oil in a large saucepan over medium heat. Add the onion, cover, and cook for 2 minutes, or until softened. Stir in the eggplant, bell pepper, and garlic. Cover and cook 5 minutes longer, stirring occasionally. Add the zucchini, tomatoes, thyme, and salt and pepper to taste. Cover and cook for 30 minutes, or until the vegetables are tender. Stir in the parsley and basil. Taste to adjust the seasoning. Serve hot.

**SERVES 4**

Per serving: 144 calories, 7 g fat, 4 g protein, 19 g carbohydrates, 7 g fiber, 0 mg cholesterol, 108 mg sodium

# CHAPTER SIX

# MAIN EVENTS

The downfall of some vegetarian diets is a tendency to rely on white rice or pasta as the focus of the meal. After all, pasta and rice dishes can be quick, tasty, and economical. While it's true that a little pasta or rice in moderation is harmless for most people, sometimes you can find yourself eating more refined carbs than anything else and ultimately putting on extra pounds—a telltale signal that it's time to reevaluate what you're eating.

Many of the recipes in this chapter are made with vegetables, beans, tofu, and nuts. Some contain whole grains such as barley, bulgur, brown rice, and quinoa. Best of all, the recipes are versatile enough to adapt to a variety of dietary choices. For example, if everyone in your household doesn't share your desire to monitor carbohydrates, a simple accompaniment of potatoes or noodles is often enough to keep the family peace. In addition, you'll find suggestions for flavorful low-carb or "good-carb" accompaniments.

# MILE-HIGH ROASTED VEGETABLES
# WITH WILD MUSHROOM SAUCE

*These towering stacks aren't really a mile high, but the deep, rich flavor of the roasted vegetables does soar to great heights. For best appearance, choose vegetables that are similar in diameter.*

1 large eggplant, cut into 8 slices about ½" thick

Olive oil

1 large sweet yellow onion, cut into 4 slices about ½" thick

1 large red bell pepper, cut into 4 rings about ½" thick

4 large portobello mushroom caps, gills removed

1 large tomato, cut into 4 slices about ½" thick

Salt and freshly ground black pepper

Wild Mushroom Sauce (page 164)

4 sprigs of fresh thyme

Preheat the oven to 400°F. Brush the eggplant slices with oil and arrange on a lightly oiled baking sheet. Bake until soft, turning once, about 20 minutes.

Brush the onion slices with oil and arrange on a separate oiled baking sheet. Bake for 10 minutes, turn the onion slices, and add the bell pepper rings to the baking sheet. Roast until the vegetables are tender, about 10 minutes for the onion and 15 minutes for the peppers.

Lightly oil the mushroom caps and place them on a baking sheet. Roast until softened, about 10 minutes.

Cool the cooked vegetables slightly, then assemble them in stacks in a lightly oiled shallow baking dish, seasoning each layer with salt and pepper: To begin, arrange the mushroom caps in the baking dish. Top each mushroom cap with a slice of eggplant, followed by a slice of onion, followed by a pepper ring. Top with another eggplant slice, followed by a slice of tomato.

Cover the baking dish with foil and reduce the oven temperature to 350°F. Bake the vegetables until hot, about 20 minutes. While the vegetables are cooking, heat the sauce.

Use a metal spatula to carefully remove the vegetable stacks from the baking dish. Place the stacks in the center of individual dinner plates. Surround each with ¼ cup of the sauce and serve hot, garnished with thyme sprigs.

**SERVES 4**

Per serving: 77 calories, 0 g fat, 3 g protein, 18 g carbohydrates, 5 g fiber, 0 mg cholesterol, 9 mg sodium

## FENNEL AND ARTICHOKE GRATIN WITH THREE-HERB WHITE BEAN PESTO

*This elegant and easy gratin tastes more indulgent than it actually is. The lean and flavorful sauce is made with pureed white beans and herbs instead of heavy cream. The traditional butter and bread crumb topping is replaced with chopped pine nuts. A light dusting of soy Parmesan is optional.*

1 tablespoon olive oil

1 leek, white part only, thinly sliced

1 yellow bell pepper, finely chopped

2 cloves garlic, finely chopped

1 large fennel bulb, thinly sliced

Salt and freshly ground black pepper

1 package (9 ounces) frozen artichoke hearts, cooked and sliced

¾ cup cooked white beans

1 cup fresh basil leaves

¼ cup chopped fresh flat-leaf parsley

¼ cup chopped fresh tarragon or savory

½ cup vegetable stock

1 tomato, cut into thin slices

¼ cup finely chopped pine nuts

Grated soy Parmesan cheese (optional)

Preheat the oven to 375°F.

Heat the oil in a large skillet over medium heat. Add the leek, bell pepper, garlic, fennel, and salt and pepper to taste. Cover and cook until the vegetables are tender, stirring occasionally, about 5 minutes.

Lightly oil a 2-quart gratin dish or coat it with cooking spray. Spread half of the fennel mixture in the bottom of the prepared dish. Top with half of the artichoke slices and season with salt and pepper. Top with the remaining fennel mixture, the remaining artichoke slices, and salt and pepper to taste.

In a blender or food processor, blend the beans, basil, parsley, and tarragon or savory until finely chopped. Add the stock and blend until smooth. Pour over the gratin. Arrange the tomato slices around the outer edge of the gratin. Sprinkle the gratin with the pine nuts and season with salt and pepper to taste.

Bake until the vegetables are tender, the top is golden brown, and the liquid is absorbed, about 1 hour. Serve directly from the gratin dish, sprinkled with Parmesan.

**SERVES 4**

Per serving: 136 calories, 4 g fat, 6 g protein, 23 g carbohydrates, 9 g fiber, 0 mg cholesterol, 290 mg sodium

**Variation:** Regular grated Parmesan cheese may be used instead of the soy Parmesan.

# CRISPY TARRAGON TOFU STRIPS WITH MUSHROOMS, LEMON, AND CAPERS

*This is a lovely, elegant way to serve tofu that is also quick and easy. If you don't have a non-stick pan, bake the tofu strips so they become crisp and golden without sticking. In fact, tofu turns out a little chewier and crispier when baked, although it does take a bit longer. To bake, place the tofu strips in an oiled baking pan and bake at 400°F for 30 minutes, turning once halfway through.*

1 pound extra-firm tofu, cut into ¼" strips
Salt and freshly ground black pepper
2 tablespoons olive oil
2 shallots, finely chopped
8 ounces white mushrooms, sliced
¼ cup dry white wine
3 tablespoons fresh lemon juice
2 tablespoon capers, rinsed, drained, and chopped
2 tablespoons finely chopped fresh tarragon or 1 teaspoon dried tarragon

Pat the tofu dry and season with salt and pepper. Heat 1 tablespoon of the oil in a large non-stick skillet over medium-high heat. Add the tofu and cook in batches until crisp and golden, 5 to 7 minutes. Remove the tofu from the pan and set aside.

Reheat the skillet over medium heat with the remaining 1 tablespoon oil. Add the shallots and cook until softened, about 2 minutes. Add the mushrooms and cook until softened, 3 to 5 minutes. Stir in the wine, lemon juice, and capers and simmer until the alcohol cooks off and the sauce reduces slightly, about 2 minutes. Return the tofu to the skillet, add the tarragon, and cook until hot.

**SERVES 4**

Per serving: 161 calories, 11 g fat, 10 g protein, 6 g carbohydrates, 1 g fiber, 0 mg cholesterol, 138 mg sodium

# THAI FIREWORKS TOFU AND BROCCOLI STIR-FRY

*Use a nonstick skillet or wok, if possible, and be sure the pan is hot to prevent the tofu from sticking to the pan. For a more substantial meal, serve over freshly cooked brown rice or quinoa.*

- 3 cups broccoli florets
- 1 tablespoon canola oil
- 1 pound extra-firm tofu, cut into ½" cubes
- 2 teaspoons toasted sesame oil
- 2 shallots, finely chopped
- 1 serrano or Thai chile pepper, seeded and finely chopped, or to taste
- 1 tablespoon finely chopped fresh ginger
- 2 tablespoons low-sodium tamari soy sauce
- ½ cup chopped Thai basil
- 2 tablespoons sesame seeds, toasted
- 2 teaspoons toasted shredded coconut (optional)

Steam the broccoli until crisp-tender and then plunge it into a bowl of ice water to stop its cooking. Drain well and set aside.

Heat the canola oil in a large skillet over medium-high heat. Working in batches, add the tofu and cook until golden brown, about 7 minutes. Remove to a platter and set aside.

To the same skillet, add the sesame oil, shallots, chile pepper, and ginger and cook until fragrant. Stir in the reserved broccoli, tamari, basil, and reserved tofu. Stir-fry to heat through. Taste to adjust the seasoning. Serve topped with the sesame seeds and coconut (if using).

## SERVES 4

Per serving: 175 calories, 12 g fat, 10 g protein, 7 g carbohydrates, 2 g fiber, 0 mg cholesterol, 327 mg sodium

# SCAMPI-STYLE OYSTER MUSHROOMS WITH SLIVERS OF NORI

*There's no shrimp in this scampi-style dish, but the oyster mushrooms and nori slivers in garlic sauce produce a striking combination on their own, with just a hint of the sea. It's delicious served over brown rice and wilted spinach.*

3 tablespoons olive oil

2 large cloves garlic, crushed

1 pound oyster mushrooms

¼ cup dry white wine

½ teaspoon salt

Freshly ground black pepper

2 tablespoons fresh lemon juice

2 tablespoons chopped fresh flat-leaf parsley

1 tablespoon finely slivered nori (see note)

Heat the oil in a large skillet over medium heat. Add the garlic and mushrooms and cook until softened, 3 to 5 minutes. Add the wine, salt, and pepper to taste and simmer until the liquid is almost evaporated, 10 to 12 minutes. Stir in the lemon juice and parsley and serve hot, sprinkled with nori.

**SERVES 4**

Per serving: 131 calories, 10 g fat, 3 g protein, 7 g carbohydrates, 1 g fiber, 0 mg cholesterol, 293 mg sodium

Note: Use scissors to cut two ½"-wide strips from a sheet of nori. Stack the strips and use scissors to cut thin crosswise slivers of nori.

# CAULIFLOWER, GREEN BEAN, AND EGGPLANT CURRY

*Cooked chickpeas or kidney beans may be used instead of or in addition to the eggplant, if you wish, to add protein, fiber, and "good" carbs.*

2 teaspoons olive oil

½ cup chopped onion

1 eggplant, cut into ½" cubes

2 cloves garlic, chopped

1 jalapeño chile pepper, seeded and finely chopped (optional)

1½ tablespoons curry powder, or to taste

1 small head cauliflower, cut into small florets

8 ounces green beans, cut into 1" pieces

1 can (14½ ounces) diced tomatoes, drained

2 cups vegetable stock

Salt and freshly ground black pepper

Heat the oil in a large pot over medium heat. Add the onion, cover, and cook until tender, about 3 minutes. Add the eggplant and garlic and cook, stirring, for 2 minutes. Cover and cook until softened, about 5 minutes. Stir in the jalapeño pepper and curry powder, then add the cauliflower, beans, tomatoes, stock, and salt and pepper to taste. Cover and bring to a boil.

Reduce the heat to low and simmer until the vegetables are tender, about 25 minutes. If a thicker sauce is desired when the vegetables are tender, use an immersion blender to break up some of the vegetables (or remove up to 2 cups of the solids and liquid from the pot, puree them in a blender or food processor, and return them to the pot).

**SERVES 4**

Per serving: 141 calories, 3 g fat, 5 g protein, 26 g carbohydrates, 10 g fiber, 0 mg cholesterol, 364 mg sodium

# EGGPLANT STUFFED WITH ZUCCHINI, CAULIFLOWER, AND SUN-DRIED TOMATOES

*This dish is a feast for veggie lovers. It's satisfying and full flavored but extremely low in carbs.*

- 1 large or 2 medium eggplants, halved lengthwise
- 1 tablespoon olive oil
- 2 scallions, chopped
- 1 clove garlic, finely chopped
- 1 zucchini, coarsely chopped
- Salt and freshly ground black pepper
- 2 cups cauliflower florets, steamed
- 2 tablespoons sun-dried tomatoes, soaked and chopped
- 1 tablespoon finely chopped fresh basil or 1 teaspoon dried basil
- 3 tablespoons ground walnuts

Preheat the oven to 375°F. Place the eggplant halves on a lightly oiled baking sheet, cut side down, and bake until partially softened, about 15 minutes. Remove from the oven and set aside to cool. When cool enough to handle, scoop out the inside of the eggplants, leaving the shells intact; set the shells aside. Coarsely chop the eggplant pulp and set aside.

Heat the oil in a large skillet over low heat. Add the scallions, garlic, zucchini, and the reserved eggplant pulp and cook until tender, about 10 minutes. Season with salt and pepper to taste. Remove from the heat to cool slightly, then stir in the cauliflower, tomatoes, and basil. Mix well. Taste to adjust the seasoning.

Spoon the stuffing mixture into the eggplant shells and arrange in a lightly oiled shallow baking dish. Sprinkle with the walnuts and salt and pepper to taste. Cover tightly and bake until tender and hot, about 30 minutes.

**SERVES 4**

Per serving: 135 calories, 6 g fat, 4 g protein, 18 g carbohydrates, 8 g fiber, 0 mg cholesterol, 62 mg sodium

# BULGUR-STUFFED BELL PEPPERS

*Colorful bell peppers hold a hearty and flavorful stuffing made with bulgur, the crushed wheat kernels that are used to prepare tabbouleh.*

4 red or yellow bell peppers, halved lengthwise and seeded
1 tablespoon olive oil
¼ cup finely chopped onion
¼ cup finely chopped celery
1 clove garlic, finely chopped
2 cups coarsely chopped white mushrooms
2 tablespoons finely chopped fresh flat-leaf parsley
½ teaspoon salt
¼ teaspoon freshly ground black pepper
2 cups cooked bulgur
1 cup tomato juice

Preheat the oven to 375°F.

Place the peppers in a pot of boiling water for 3 to 4 minutes to soften slightly. Drain and set aside.

Heat the oil in a large skillet over medium heat. Add the onion and celery, cover, and cook until softened, about 5 minutes. Add the garlic and mushrooms and cook until tender, about 5 minutes. Add the parsley, salt, and pepper.

Transfer to a large bowl and stir in the bulgur. Taste to adjust the seasoning. Stuff the peppers with the filling and place in a lightly oiled baking dish. Pour the tomato juice over all and cover with foil. Bake until the peppers are tender, about 30 minutes.

**SERVES 4**

Per serving: 176 calories, 4 g fat, 7 g protein, 32 g carbohydrates, 8 g fiber, 0 mg cholesterol, 473 mg sodium

# SPINACH PIE WITH WALNUT CRUST

*The walnut crust is an ideal complement to the spinach filling. It's also simple to make, loaded with flavor, and much better for you than a traditional white flour crust.*

1½ cups walnut pieces

¼ cup grated soy Parmesan cheese

1 pound spinach, tough stems removed

1 tablespoon olive oil

¼ cup finely chopped onion

2 cloves garlic, finely chopped

1 pound firm tofu, crumbled

1 tablespoon fresh lemon juice

1 teaspoon salt

¼ teaspoon freshly ground black pepper

Pinch of ground nutmeg

Preheat the oven to 350°F.

Finely grind the walnuts in a food processor. Add the Parmesan and pulse to combine. Transfer the mixture to a 9" pie plate, press into the bottom and sides, and set aside.

Steam the spinach until tender, about 3 minutes. Squeeze out any moisture, coarsely chop, and set aside.

Heat the oil in a large skillet over medium heat. Add the onion, cover, and cook until tender, 3 minutes. Add the garlic and cook until fragrant, 30 seconds. Add the reserved spinach and cook until any liquid is absorbed. Then transfer to a food processor. Add the tofu, lemon juice, salt, pepper, and nutmeg and process until well combined.

Spread the filling mixture in the prepared crust and smooth the top. Bake until golden brown, about 60 minutes. Let stand 10 minutes before cutting. Serve warm or at room temperature.

**SERVES 4**

Per serving: 460 calories, 40 g fat, 20 g protein, 14 g carbohydrates, 6 g fiber, 0 mg cholesterol, 832 mg sodium

**Variation:** Regular grated Parmesan cheese may be used instead of the soy Parmesan.

# THREE-RICE PILAF

*Wild rice is actually a grass, and the shredded cauliflower just resembles rice, making the brown rice the only authentic rice here. No matter. This pilaf is lovely, delicious, and special enough for a festive meal.*

2 tablespoons olive oil

1 large shallot, finely chopped

1 teaspoon finely chopped fresh ginger

½ cup wild rice

¼ teaspoon ground cumin

¼ teaspoon ground coriander

⅛ teaspoon ground red pepper

2½ cups hot water

Salt and freshly ground black pepper

½ cup brown rice

3 cups shredded cauliflower, steamed until just tender

¼ cup slivered almonds, toasted

2 tablespoons finely chopped fresh flat-leaf parsley

Heat the oil in a large skillet over medium heat. Add the shallot and ginger and cook until the shallot is slightly softened, about 1 minute. Add the wild rice, cumin, coriander, and ground red pepper and stir to coat with the oil. Stir in the water and bring to a boil. Reduce the heat to low and season to taste with salt and pepper.

Cover and cook for 15 minutes. Add the brown rice and continue cooking until the water is absorbed and the rices are tender, about 45 minutes longer. Remove from the heat and stir in the cauliflower, almonds, and parsley.

**SERVES 6**

Per serving: 183 calories, 7 g fat, 5 g protein, 26 g carbohydrates, 3 g fiber, 0 mg cholesterol, 18 mg sodium

# JAMAICAN ROASTED VEGETABLES

*The fragrant spices may conjure up images of the islands when you bite into these delicious baked vegetables. You can vary the vegetables according to preference and cook them on the grill, if you like.*

    2 teaspoons dried thyme
    1 teaspoon ground allspice
    1 teaspoon salt
    Pinch of stevia
    ½ teaspoon ground paprika
    ⅛ teaspoon ground red pepper, or to taste
    ¼ teaspoon ground nutmeg
    ¼ teaspoon freshly ground black pepper
    4 shallots, halved or quartered
    1 large red or yellow bell pepper, cut into large dice
    4 portobello mushroom caps, gills removed and caps cut into 1" strips
    2 zucchini, cut into ½" slices
    2 tablespoons olive oil

Preheat the oven to 400°F.

In a small bowl, combine the thyme, allspice, salt, stevia, paprika, ground red pepper, nutmeg, and black pepper.

Place the shallots, bell pepper, mushrooms, and zucchini in a large bowl and toss them with the oil to coat. Sprinkle with the spice mixture, stirring to coat. Transfer the vegetables to a lightly oiled baking dish, cover, and roast until the vegetables are tender, about 30 minutes. Remove the cover and roast for 10 minutes longer to brown.

**SERVES 4**

Per serving: 110 calories, 7 g fat, 4 g protein, 10 g carbohydrates, 3 g fiber, 0 mg cholesterol, 586 mg sodium

# BLACK BEAN AND SESAME-STUFFED
# PORTOBELLO MUSHROOMS

*These mushrooms are so easy to prepare that you'll want to make them often. They're so flavorful and appealing on the plate, you'll even want to serve them to company.*

> 2 tablespoons canola oil
>
> 4 large portobello mushroom caps, gills removed
>
> Salt and freshly ground black pepper
>
> 1 clove garlic, chopped
>
> 1 red bell pepper, chopped
>
> 1 teaspoon finely chopped fresh ginger
>
> 2 cups cooked black beans
>
> 3 tablespoons tahini paste
>
> 3 tablespoons finely chopped fresh cilantro
>
> 1 tablespoon low-sodium tamari soy sauce
>
> 1 teaspoon toasted sesame oil
>
> 2 teaspoons sesame seeds

Preheat the oven to 375°F.

Heat 1 tablespoon of the canola oil in a large skillet over medium-high heat. Add the mushrooms, gill side up. Sear until browned, about 30 seconds. Turn over, season with salt and pepper, and cook 30 seconds longer. Remove the mushrooms from the skillet and set aside.

Reheat the same skillet with the remaining 1 tablespoon canola oil over medium heat. Add the garlic and bell pepper and cook until softened, about 5 minutes. Stir in the ginger, beans, tahini, cilantro, tamari, and sesame oil. Cook, stirring, for 1 minute to combine and blend the flavors. Remove from the heat and set aside until cool enough to handle.

Press about ½ cup of the stuffing mixture into each mushroom cap and sprinkle with the sesame seeds. Place the stuffed mushrooms in a lightly oiled baking dish. Cover and bake until the filling is hot and the mushrooms are tender, about 25 minutes.

**SERVES 4**

Per serving: 284 calories, 16 g fat, 12 g protein, 24 g carbohydrates, 9 g fiber, 0 mg cholesterol, 556 mg sodium

# ROASTED EGGPLANT LASAGNA WITH WINTERTIME SPINACH PESTO

*Thinly sliced layers of roasted eggplant replace the noodles in this flavorful lasagna that has the added taste of spinach pesto.*

2 large eggplants, peeled and thinly sliced lengthwise

2 tablespoons olive oil

Salt and freshly ground black pepper

2 pounds firm tofu, well drained

¼ cup finely chopped fresh flat-leaf parsley

¼ cup grated soy Parmesan cheese

1½ cups marinara or other tomato sauce, bottled or homemade

1 cup Wintertime Spinach Pesto (page 161)

1 cup shredded soy mozzarella cheese

Preheat the oven to 425°F. Arrange the eggplant slices on lightly oiled baking sheets. Brush with oil and season with salt and pepper. Bake until tender and lightly browned around the edges, turning once, about 10 minutes total. Set aside.

Reduce the oven temperature to 350°F.

Crumble the tofu into a large bowl and add the parsley, Parmesan, and salt and pepper to taste; blend well.

In the bottom of a 13" × 9" baking dish, spread a thin layer of tomato sauce and top with a layer of the eggplant slices. Spread half of the tofu mixture over the eggplant and top with half of the pesto. Spread some tomato sauce on top and add another layer of eggplant slices. Spread on the remaining tofu mixture; top with the remaining pesto and the remaining eggplant. Top with tomato sauce and the mozzarella.

Bake for 45 minutes, or until bubbly. Remove from the oven and let stand for 15 minutes before cutting.

SERVES 6

Per serving: 271 calories, 16 g fat, 18 g protein, 18 g carbohydrates, 5 g fiber, 0 mg cholesterol, 425 mg sodium

**Variation:** Regular dairy Parmesan and mozzarella cheeses may be used instead of the soy cheeses.

## SPECIALTY PRODUCT BRANDS

In recent years, numerous brands of soy products and other vegetarian meat alternatives have appeared on the market. Here are a few of the most widely available brands and just a sampling of their products.

**Boca Food Co.**
Phone: 608–285–3311
www.bocaburger.com

- Burgers, including Vegan, Roasted Onion, and All-American Classic
- Lasagna; pizza with meatless sausage and pepperoni
- Breakfast patties and links; sausages and bratwurst
- Chick'n patties and nuggets

**Yves Veggie Cuisine, Inc.**
Phone: 800–667–9837
www.yvesveggie.com

- Breakfast foods, including Canadian Veggie Bacon and Veggie Breakfast Links
- Veggie burgers and dogs
- Deli bologna, ham, and turkey slices; cheese slices

**Lightlife Foods**
Phone: 800–soy–easy
www.lightlife.com

- Smart Menu deli slices, links, brats, tofu pups
- Gimme Lean bulk-style sausage and ground beef
- Organic tempeh
- Smart Menu Steak-Style Strips and Chick'n Strips

# PORTOBELLO PATTIES WITH CHARMOULA SAUCE

*The lemony Moroccan charmoula sauce is a luscious complement to the flavors in the mushroom patties. This recipe makes a delicious entrée, but you can also roll the mushroom mixture into 1" balls, bake them, and serve them as appetizers with the sauce.*

8 ounces portobello mushroom caps, gills removed

8 ounces Gimme Lean ground beef alternative

¼ cup finely chopped onion

1 clove garlic, finely chopped

2 tablespoons chopped fresh cilantro

1 tablespoon chopped fresh mint or 1 teaspoon dried mint

½ teaspoon ground cumin

½ teaspoon ground ginger

¾ teaspoon salt

½ teaspoon freshly ground black pepper

Olive oil

Charmoula Sauce (page 171)

Grind the portobellos in a food processor and combine with the beef alternative, onion, garlic, cilantro, mint, cumin, ginger, salt, and pepper. Mix well, then refrigerate in a covered container for 1 to 2 hours to allow the flavors to blend together.

Preheat the grill or broiler (or set the oven at 375°F). Shape the mixture into patties, brush with a small amount of oil, and grill or broil until browned, about 3 minutes per side (or bake until browned, about 10 minutes). Serve with the sauce.

### SERVES 4

Per serving: 95 calories, 0 g fat, 11 g protein, 13 g carbohydrates, 2 g fiber, 0 mg cholesterol, 678 mg sodium

# SLOPPY JOSEPHINES

*This variation on Sloppy Joes tastes even better the next day, so make it the night before for a no-fuss lunch. You can serve it on whole grain or low-carb rolls or in pita pockets. Or do as I sometimes do: Serve it on a bed of shredded lettuce or as a tasty topping to spaghetti squash.*

1 tablespoon olive oil

¼ cup finely chopped onion

½ cup chopped red bell pepper

2 cups ground portobello mushrooms

Salt and freshly ground black pepper

1 package (12 ounces) frozen vegetarian burgers, thawed and chopped
   (see note)

¾ cup tomato sauce

1 teaspoon yellow or Dijon mustard

½ teaspoon agave syrup or a pinch of stevia (optional)

Heat the oil in a large skillet over medium-high heat. Add the onion and bell pepper, cover, and cook until the vegetables are soft, about 5 minutes. Add the mushrooms and salt and pepper to taste. Cook for 3 minutes, stirring occasionally. Stir in the vegetarian burgers, tomato sauce, mustard, and agave syrup or stevia. Simmer for 10 minutes, until the flavors are blended and the mixture is hot.

## SERVES 4

Per serving: 182 calories, 7 g fat, 14 g protein, 18 g carbohydrates, 8 g fiber, 0 mg cholesterol, 596 mg sodium

Note: You may replace the burgers with frozen vegetarian burger crumbles.

## SPAGHETTI SQUASH AND SNOW PEAS WITH PEANUT SAUCE

*If you'd rather not cut into the hard spaghetti squash, you can cook it whole. Just pierce it several times with a fork and bake until soft. It will then be easier to cut it open and scoop out the seeds.*

- ⅓ cup creamy reduced-fat peanut butter
- 1 teaspoon finely chopped garlic
- 3 tablespoons low-sodium tamari soy sauce
- ⅓ cup water
- 1 tablespoon rice vinegar
- ½ teaspoon red-pepper flakes (optional)
- 1 spaghetti squash, halved crosswise
- 1 cup snow peas
- 2 tablespoons fresh cilantro, finely chopped
- 1 tablespoon chopped roasted peanuts (optional)

Preheat the oven to 375°F.

In a small bowl or food processor, mix the peanut butter, garlic, tamari, water, vinegar, and red-pepper flakes (if using) until well blended. Taste to adjust the seasoning. Add more water if necessary to make a smooth and creamy sauce. Set aside.

Place the squash halves, cut side up, in a baking dish. Add an inch or so of water to the dish and cover tightly with a lid or foil. Bake until tender, 45 minutes to 1 hour.

Just before serving time, steam the snow peas until just tender, about 2 minutes. Remove and discard the seeds from the squash. Use a fork to flake the squash into strands and place the strands in a large bowl. Add the reserved peanut sauce and the snow peas and toss gently to combine. Sprinkle with cilantro and chopped peanuts (if using).

**SERVES 4**

Per serving: 231 calories, 12 g fat, 9 g protein, 26 g carbohydrates, 6 g fiber, 0 mg cholesterol, 527 mg sodium

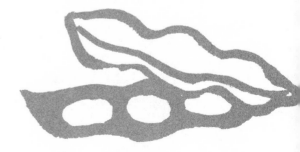

## CARROT AND ZUCCHINI "LINGUINE" WITH EDAMAME, BLACK OLIVES, AND ARUGULA PESTO

*This colorful dish is almost as much fun to make as it is to eat. Unlike the empty carbs of refined white pasta, this vegetable "linguine" is loaded with important nutrients. There are a number of kitchen tools available to achieve long strands of vegetables, ranging from the expensive mandoline slicer to less-expensive plastic gadgets. When all else fails, a simple vegetable peeler can get the job done.*

6 zucchini

2 large carrots

2 cups fresh or frozen shelled edamame, cooked

1 cup Arugula Pesto (page 162)

¼ cup chopped kalamata olives

Separately trim and cut the zucchini and the carrots into long thin strips, using a mandoline or vegetable peeler. Steam the zucchini strips until tender, 3 to 5 minutes. Steam the carrot strips until tender, 5 to 7 minutes. In a shallow bowl, combine the zucchini and carrots with the edamame and pesto and toss gently to combine. Sprinkle with the olives and serve hot.

SERVES 4

Per serving: 562 calories, 39 g fat, 30 g protein, 28 g carbohydrates, 10 g fiber, 0 mg cholesterol, 643 mg sodium

# BURGUNDY-LACED RED BEANS AND MUSHROOMS

*The juicy mushrooms absorb the rich flavor of the wine sauce that gives this humble bean dish a touch of class. Serve it over Cauliflower "Mashed Potatoes" (page 111), Three-Rice Pilaf (page 130), or freshly cooked brown rice.*

1 tablespoon olive oil

2 shallots, quartered

1 clove garlic, finely chopped

12 ounces white mushrooms, quartered

1 tablespoon tomato paste

2 teaspoons finely chopped fresh thyme or ½ teaspoon dried thyme

2 bay leaves

1¼ cups vegetable stock

¾ cup dry red wine

2 cups cooked kidney beans

Salt and freshly ground black pepper

Heat the oil in a large skillet over medium heat. Add the shallots and cook until lightly browned, about 5 minutes. Stir in the garlic and cook until fragrant, about 30 seconds. Remove the shallots and garlic from the skillet and set aside.

Add the mushrooms to the same skillet and cook until they release their juices, about 3 minutes. Remove the mushrooms from the skillet and set aside.

In the same skillet, stir together the tomato paste, thyme, bay leaves, and stock. Bring to a boil, then reduce the heat to low. Add the reserved shallots, cover, and simmer until tender, about 10 minutes. Stir in the wine, beans, and salt and pepper to taste. Return to a boil, then reduce the heat to low. Add the reserved mushrooms and simmer, uncovered, 10 minutes more. Remove and discard the bay leaves before serving.

## SERVES 4

Per serving: 210 calories, 4 g fat, 11 g protein, 27 g carbohydrates, 10 g fiber, 0 mg cholesterol, 429 mg sodium

# SINLESS SHEPHERD'S PIE

*You can indulge in this homestyle favorite without guilt because the buttery rich top layer is made with mashed cauliflower instead of potatoes. Mushrooms and vegetarian burger crumbles replace traditional ground beef. Look for frozen vegetarian burger crumbles in large supermarkets and natural food stores.*

8 ounces green beans, cut into ½" pieces

1 small carrot, chopped

1 tablespoon olive oil

½ cup finely chopped onion

1 zucchini, chopped

1 yellow summer squash, chopped

6 ounces white mushrooms, chopped

1½ cups vegetarian burger crumbles

2 cups Wild Mushroom Sauce (page 164)

1 tablespoon low-sodium tamari soy sauce

½ teaspoon finely chopped fresh thyme or ¼ teaspoon dried thyme

Salt and freshly ground black pepper

1 head cauliflower, cut into 1" pieces

1 tablespoon nonhydrogenated, trans-free margarine

Preheat the oven to 375°F.

Cook the beans and carrot in a saucepan of boiling salted water until tender, about 7 minutes. Drain and set aside.

Heat the oil in a large skillet over medium heat. Add the onion, cover, and cook until soft, about 5 minutes. Add the zucchini, squash, and mushrooms; cover and cook for 5 minutes longer. Stir in the reserved beans and carrot, the burger crumbles, mushroom sauce, tamari, thyme, and salt and pepper to taste. Spoon into a lightly oiled shallow baking dish.

Steam the cauliflower until soft, about 10 minutes. Transfer to a bowl, add the margarine and salt to taste, and mash until smooth. (You can also do this in a food processor, if you prefer.) Spread the mashed cauliflower on top of the vegetable mixture, smoothing to cover the surface. Bake until heated through and golden on top, about 30 minutes.

**SERVES 6**

Per serving: 143 calories, 6 g fat, 9 g protein, 16 g carbohydrates, 7 g fiber, 0 mg cholesterol, 266 mg sodium

**Variation:** Butter may be used instead of the margarine.

## GLYCEMIC LOAD AND THE TRUTH ABOUT CARROTS

Carrots are low in calories and have no fat or cholesterol, so they've long been considered a perfect "diet" food. Then along came the *glycemic index,* which scored carrots undesirably high on the list (between 75 and 90, depending on the source).

At first glance, then, you might think you need to give up carrots. Here's where the *glycemic load* comes to their rescue. The glycemic load shows how much a certain food raises blood sugar. A value of 10 or less is considered good, and the great news is that carrots have a glycemic load of less than 5. In fact, despite carrots' high glycemic index value, one raw carrot contains only 7.3 grams of carbohydrates; ½ cup of cooked carrots has just 6 grams of carbohydrates. More carrots, anyone?

# SPICE-RUBBED VEGETABLE KEBABS

*If you like to grill a lot of veggies, make a big batch of this spice rub to keep on hand. These kebabs can be cooked on an outdoor grill as well as in an indoor grill, broiler, or even a hot oven. If using wooden bamboo skewers, soak them in water for 30 minutes beforehand to keep them from burning.*

½ teaspoon salt

¼ teaspoon freshly ground black pepper

¼ teaspoon dried thyme

¼ teaspoon onion powder

¼ teaspoon garlic powder

¼ teaspoon ground fennel seeds

¼ teaspoon ground allspice

¼ teaspoon ground red pepper

8 large scallions or 4 shallots

1 red bell pepper, halved

2 small zucchini or yellow summer squash

8 white mushrooms

1 fennel bulb, quartered and separated into 8 pieces

8 cherry tomatoes

2 tablespoons olive oil

Preheat the grill or broiler or turn the oven to 450°F.

In a small bowl, combine the salt, pepper, thyme, onion powder, garlic powder, fennel seeds, allspice, and ground red pepper. Mix well and set aside.

Remove most of the green part of the scallions and reserve for another use, leaving the white part and enough green to make a 3" piece (or halve the shallots, if using). Quarter the bell pepper halves to make 8 pieces. Cut the zucchini or squash into 8 bite-size chunks, approximately 1" long.

Place the scallions or shallots, bell pepper, zucchini or squash, mushrooms, fennel pieces, and tomatoes in a bowl and drizzle with the oil. Sprinkle with the reserved spice blend, turning the vegetables to coat.

Thread 1 piece of each vegetable onto 8 skewers. Cook on a grill until the vegetables are tender, turning once, about 10 minutes. (Alternatively, place the skewers on a lightly oiled baking sheet and broil or bake until tender.)

**SERVES 4**

Per serving: 122 calories, 7 g fat, 3 g protein, 13 g carbohydrates, 5 g fiber, 0 mg cholesterol, 331 mg sodium

# VERY VEGGIE BURGERS WITH "BASIC BLACK" BEAN SAUCE

*Protein-rich lentils, walnuts, and tahini combine with whole grain oats and vegetables for tasty burgers that pack a nutritional wallop.*

1 tablespoon olive oil

1 small onion, finely chopped

1 zucchini, grated

1 cup chopped white mushrooms

½ cup ground walnuts

1 tablespoon finely chopped fresh flat-leaf parsley

1 cup cooked brown lentils, well drained

2 tablespoons tahini paste

1 teaspoon low-sodium tamari soy sauce

½ cup rolled oats, finely ground

Salt and freshly ground black pepper

"Basic Black" Bean Sauce (page 165)

Heat the oil in a large skillet over medium heat. Add the onion, zucchini, and mushrooms and cook until soft, 5 minutes. Transfer to a large bowl. Add the walnuts and parsley; set aside.

Pulse the lentils in a food processor until coarsely chopped and add to the bowl. In the food processor, blend the tahini, tamari, and oats until mixed well; stir into the bowl and mix well. Season with salt and pepper to taste.

Use parchment or waxed paper to shape the mixture into 4 patties and place them on a plate. Refrigerate for 30 minutes to chill.

Preheat the oven to 350°F. Arrange the patties on a lightly oiled baking sheet. Bake until hot and lightly browned, turning once, about 30 minutes. Serve with the sauce.

**SERVES 4**

Per serving: 299 calories, 19 g fat, 12 g protein, 26 g carbohydrates, 8 g fiber, 0 mg cholesterol, 166 mg sodium

# THREE-BEAN CAKES

*If you like three-bean salad, you'll enjoy these three-bean cakes, made with green beans, lentils, and kidney beans (or substitute a different bean that you have on hand). The cakes have a nice crispy texture on the outside and are soft and flavorful on the inside. Serve them with a brown sauce, black bean sauce, or even curry sauce.*

½ cup rolled oats
¾ cup cooked kidney beans
¾ cup cooked lentils
1 cup cooked green beans cut into 1" pieces
½ cup chopped walnuts or pecans
½ cup chopped onion
2–3 cloves garlic
2½ tablespoons tahini paste
1 tablespoon finely chopped fresh flat-leaf parsley
Salt and freshly ground black pepper

Process the oats in a food processor until fine. Add the kidney beans, lentils, green beans, walnuts or pecans, onion, and garlic; process until well combined. Add the tahini, parsley, and salt and pepper to taste. Pulse until the mixture is well combined.

Use parchment or waxed paper to shape the mixture into 4 patties and place them on a plate. Refrigerate for 30 minutes to chill.

Preheat the oven to 350°F. Arrange the patties on a lightly oiled baking sheet. Bake until hot and lightly browned, turning once, about 30 minutes.

**SERVES 4**

Per serving: 298 calories, 16 g fat, 12 g protein, 30 g carbohydrates, 11 g fiber, 0 mg cholesterol, 198 mg sodium

# VIRTUOUS VEGETABLE TAGINE

*A classic Moroccan dish, tagine is the name of both the stew and the clay pot in which the stew is cooked. Traditionally, tagine contains a variety of dried fruits (which are not low carb) and meats (which are not vegetarian) and is often served over couscous (which is not a whole grain). This version, containing no meat and only a miniscule amount of dried fruit, is delicious served over freshly cooked brown rice, quinoa, or other whole grains.*

1 tablespoon olive oil

½ cup chopped onion

1 red bell pepper, chopped

1 clove garlic, chopped

1 teaspoon finely chopped fresh ginger

2 tablespoons tomato paste

½ teaspoon ground cinnamon

½ teaspoon ground cumin

½ teaspoon ground paprika

½ teaspoon ground turmeric

1 tablespoon fresh lemon juice

Salt and freshly ground black pepper

2 cups vegetable stock

1 large eggplant, cut into cubes

8 ounces green beans, cut into 1" pieces

¼ cup pitted imported green olives

2 tablespoons finely chopped fresh cilantro or flat-leaf parsley

1 tablespoon golden raisins or finely chopped dried apricots

Heat the oil in a large saucepan over medium heat. Add the onion and bell pepper; cover and cook for 5 minutes. Stir in the garlic, ginger, tomato paste, cinnamon, cumin, paprika, turmeric, lemon juice, and salt and pepper to taste. Add the stock, eggplant, and beans and bring to a boil.

Reduce the heat to low and simmer, covered, until the vegetables are tender, 20 to 30 minutes. Stir in the olives, cilantro or parsley, and raisins or apricots and cook 5 minutes longer. Taste to adjust the seasoning.

**SERVES 4**

Per serving: 137 calories, 5 g fat, 3 g protein, 22 g carbohydrates, 8 g fiber, 0 mg cholesterol, 315 mg sodium

## THE GRAIN IMPOSTOR

A great number of grains can boost your fiber while delivering protein and other nutrients. You may already have many of them in your pantry: barley, bulgur, brown rice, quinoa, and oatmeal, for example. But what about couscous? Sorry, but as tasty and popular as it is, couscous has just been masquerading as a grain. In reality, it is a tiny pasta. Made from semolina, couscous is not whole grain and therefore not a whole food. So, when choosing your "good" carbs, either forgo this grain impostor altogether or select the healthier whole wheat version.

## SPAGHETTI SQUASH WITH FRESH TOMATO SAUCE

*Make this tomato sauce when you're looking for a way to use ripe tomatoes. It's a fast and fresh way to enjoy cooked spaghetti squash. Note: The spaghetti squash can be cooked whole if you prefer. Pierce it in several places with a fork and bake until tender. It will take a bit longer to cook, but it eliminates the precarious job of cutting into a hard squash.*

2 tablespoons olive oil

1 tablespoon balsamic vinegar

5–6 plum tomatoes, chopped

¼ cup sliced kalamata olives

¼ cup sliced green olives

¼ cup finely chopped scallions

¼ cup finely chopped fresh flat-leaf parsley

1 tablespoon capers, rinsed, drained, and chopped

Red-pepper flakes (optional)

Salt and freshly ground black pepper

1 large spaghetti squash, halved crosswise

Preheat the oven to 375°F.

In a medium bowl, whisk together the oil and vinegar, then stir in the tomatoes, kalamata olives, green olives, scallions, parsley, capers, and red-pepper flakes (if using). Add salt and pepper to taste. Set aside and allow the flavors to mingle while you cook the squash.

Place the squash halves, cut side up, in a baking dish. Add an inch or so of water to the dish and cover tightly with a lid or foil. Bake until tender, 45 minutes to 1 hour. Remove and discard the seeds from the squash. Use a fork to flake the squash into strands and place the strands in a large bowl. Add the reserved sauce and toss gently to combine and warm the sauce.

### SERVES 4

Per serving: 177 calories, 10 g fat, 3 g protein, 23 g carbohydrates, 5 g fiber, 0 mg cholesterol, 263 mg sodium

# GINGER-SHERRY TOFU WITH GREEN BEANS
# AND WATER CHESTNUTS

*This dish has it all: crisp, fresh vegetables and protein-rich tofu, cooked in an out-of-this-world sauce made with fresh ginger, tamari, and sherry.*

3 tablespoons low-sodium tamari soy sauce

2 tablespoons medium-dry sherry

1 tablespoon finely chopped fresh ginger

1 pound extra-firm tofu, patted dry and cut into ½" cubes

8 ounces green beans, cut into 1" pieces

1 tablespoon canola oil

2 scallions, finely chopped

½ cup canned sliced water chestnuts, drained and rinsed

In a shallow bowl, combine the tamari, sherry, and ginger. Add the tofu, stir to coat, and set aside to marinate at room temperature for 20 minutes, stirring once about halfway through.

Steam the beans until just tender, 5 to 7 minutes. Drain and rinse under cold water. Set aside.

Heat the oil in a large skillet over medium-high heat. Add the scallions and water chestnuts and cook, stirring, for 1 minute. Add the tofu with the marinade and the beans; cook, stirring gently, until hot, 5 to 7 minutes.

**SERVES 4**

Per serving: 140 calories, 8 g fat, 9 g protein, 10 g carbohydrates, 3 g fiber, 0 mg cholesterol, 15 mg sodium

# ZUCCHINI FETTUCCINE PUTTANESCA

*The goal here is to get the zucchini to look like fettuccine. You can do this by shredding the zucchini with a mandoline slicer or a Benriner slicer or by cutting it into thin strands with a good sharp chef's knife. Whatever method you use, make long, thin slivers of zucchini, so that when it is cooked until limp, it will appear like strands of pasta.*

4–6 zucchini, cut into long, thin strips
1 tablespoon olive oil
3 cloves garlic, finely chopped
2 cups finely diced fresh or canned tomatoes
¾ cup kalamata or gaeta olives, pitted and halved
¼ cup green olives, pitted and halved
2 tablespoons capers, rinsed, drained, and chopped
½ teaspoon dried basil
¼ teaspoon red-pepper flakes, or to taste (optional)
3 tablespoons finely chopped fresh flat-leaf parsley
Salt and freshly ground black pepper

Steam the zucchini strips until tender, about 5 minutes. Set aside.

Heat the oil in a large skillet over medium heat. Add the garlic and cook until fragrant, being careful not to burn it, about 30 seconds. Stir in the tomatoes, olives, capers, basil, red-pepper flakes (if using), parsley, and salt and pepper to taste. Add the reserved zucchini and cook until heated through, tossing gently to coat the zucchini with the sauce.

**SERVES 4**

Per serving: 68 calories, 5 g fat, 1 g protein, 5 g carbohydrates, 2 g fiber, 0 mg cholesterol, 282 mg sodium

# SUMMER SQUASH "PAGLIA E FIENO" WITH CREAMY CASHEW SAUCE

*Named after Tuscany's "straw and hay" pasta dish made with green and yellow noodles, this low-carb version is made with long strips of zucchini and yellow squash. To cut the squash into strips, enlist the aid of a mandoline slicer, vegetable peeler, or sharp knife.*

3 zucchini, cut into long, thin strips

3 yellow summer squash, cut into long, thin strips

2 cups Creamy Cashew Sauce (page 166)

Vegetable stock or soy milk (optional)

Freshly ground black pepper

2 tablespoons grated soy Parmesan cheese

2 tablespoons finely chopped fresh flat-leaf parsley

Steam the zucchini and squash strips until tender, about 5 to 7 minutes. Set aside.

Warm the cashew sauce in a large saucepan or deep skillet over low heat, stirring often. Add the zucchini and squash and stir gently until heated through. (If the sauce is too thick, add a little vegetable stock or milk to reach the desired consistency.) Taste to adjust the seasoning. When hot, serve at once, sprinkled with pepper to taste, Parmesan, and parsley.

## SERVES 4

Per serving: 171 calories, 7 g fat, 8 g protein, 15 g carbohydrates, 6 g fiber, 0 mg cholesterol, 282 mg sodium

**Variation:** Regular dairy Parmesan cheese may be used instead of the soy Parmesan.

# WHITE BEAN AND CHARD-STUFFED ZUCCHINI WITH RED PEPPER COULIS

*When I was a kid, we called these stuffed zucchini "boats." But with sophisticated ingredients such as chard, pine nuts, and red pepper coulis, I think we may call this version "zucchini yachts."*

4 medium zucchini, halved lengthwise

2 teaspoons olive oil

1 large clove garlic, finely chopped

1½ cups cooked Swiss chard

1 cup cooked white beans

¼ cup pine nuts, toasted

2 tablespoons finely chopped fresh flat-leaf parsley

2 tablespoons finely chopped fresh basil

Salt and freshly ground black pepper

2 tablespoons grated soy Parmesan cheese

1 cup Red Pepper Coulis (page 168)

Preheat the oven to 350°F.

Use a teaspoon to scoop out the zucchini pulp, keeping the shells intact. Chop the pulp and reserve. Steam the zucchini shells until just tender. Set aside to cool.

Heat the oil in a large skillet over medium heat. Add the garlic and zucchini pulp and cook until tender, about 5 minutes. Remove from the heat and stir in the chard, beans, pine nuts, parsley, basil, and salt and pepper to taste. Mix well. Fill the zucchini shells with the stuffing mixture and place them in a lightly oiled baking dish. Sprinkle with the Parmesan.

Cover tightly and bake until hot, about 30 minutes. To serve, spoon the coulis onto individual plates or a serving platter and place the stuffed zucchini on top.

**SERVES 4**

Per serving: 205 calories, 12 g fat, 10 g protein, 22 g carbohydrates, 2 g fiber, 0 mg cholesterol, 304 mg sodium

**Variation:** Regular dairy Parmesan cheese may be used instead of the soy cheese.

# MANY-VEGETABLE BULGUR PILAF

*Bulgur, or cracked wheat, is a hearty, quick-cooking grain made popular in the tabbouleh salad from the Middle East. Here it is combined with a variety of vegetables and chickpeas for a robust one-dish meal. Vary the vegetables and beans according to preference and availability.*

2 tablespoons olive oil

2 tablespoons chopped onion

2 red bell peppers, chopped

½ head cabbage, finely chopped

2 zucchini, coarsely chopped

1 clove garlic, finely chopped

2¼ cups water

1 cup bulgur

½ cup cooked chickpeas

¼ teaspoon ground red pepper

Salt and freshly ground black pepper

Heat the oil in a large skillet over medium heat. Add the onion, cover, and cook until softened, about 3 minutes. Stir in the bell pepper, cabbage, zucchini, and garlic. Cover and cook until softened, about 5 minutes. Stir in the water, bulgur, chickpeas, ground red pepper, and salt and pepper to taste.

Bring to a boil, then reduce the heat to low and simmer 5 minutes longer. Remove from the heat and let stand, covered, for 10 minutes, or until the liquid is absorbed by the bulgur. Fluff with a fork. Serve in a large shallow bowl.

**SERVES 6**

Per serving: 176 calories, 5 g fat, 6 g protein, 29 g carbohydrates, 0 mg cholesterol, 77 mg sodium

## BULGUR BASICS

Bulgur is whole grain wheat that has been steamed, dried, and crushed. It comes in fine, medium, or coarse grinds. Its nutty flavor and chewy texture make it an ideal choice for pilafs.

# CHAPTER SEVEN

# SAUCES, DRESSINGS, AND CONDIMENTS

Adding just the right sauce to a dish can mean the difference between a so-so meal and a spectacular one. Oftentimes, however, there are loads of hidden carbs lurking in our favorite sauces. In addition, vegetarians and others looking for cholesterol-free foods will want to avoid the butter, eggs, and dairy so prevalent in many classic sauces. Before you wonder if there's anything left to sauce your food, let me assure you that an astounding array of flavorful low-carb, cholesterol-free sauces, dressings, and condiments can be made with vegetables, beans, and nuts.

This chapter begins with a trio of pestos that couldn't be more different. All work beautifully on veggie "pasta," whole grains, and roasted vegetables or as flavorings for soups and salads.

Protein-rich Creamy Cashew Sauce, Spicy Peanut Sauce, and "Basic Black" Bean Sauce can add nutrition and flavor to vegetable "pasta," whole grain dishes, veggie burgers, and tofu.

A zesty salsa, a creamy mustard sauce, and a fiery harissa sauce round out the chapter, along with colorful Red Pepper Coulis and two lemony toppings: piquant Moroccan Charmoula Sauce and Heart-Healthy Hollandaise. There are also a number of vibrant salad dressings to drizzle onto your greens.

# RICH MAN'S PESTO

*The title comes from the fact that "poor man's pesto" referred to a pesto sauce that did not include cheese. But this version is rich in healthful ingredients without the added cholesterol that cheese would contribute.*

**2–3 cloves garlic**
**½ teaspoon salt**
**3 cups fresh basil leaves**
**⅓ cup pine nuts or walnuts**
**⅓ cup olive oil**
**Freshly ground black pepper**

In a food processor, combine the garlic and salt and process until the garlic is chopped. Add the basil and pine nuts or walnuts and process until finely chopped. Add the oil and pepper to taste and process until smooth. If not using the pesto sauce immediately, transfer it to a container, top it with a thin layer of olive oil, cover it tightly to prevent browning, and refrigerate.

**MAKES ABOUT 1 CUP**

Per 2 tablespoons: 116 calories, 12 g fat, 2 g protein, 2 g carbohydrates, 1 g fiber, 0 mg cholesterol, 146 mg sodium

# WINTERTIME SPINACH PESTO

*This is a good choice when you crave pesto sauce but fresh basil is unavailable. A great thing about this pesto (in addition to the iron and other nutrients from the spinach) is that it remains a bright green color.*

3 cups fresh spinach, chopped

1 cup chopped fresh flat-leaf parsley

2 teaspoons dried basil

2 cloves garlic, chopped

¼ cup pine nuts

3 tablespoons olive oil

3 tablespoons grated soy Parmesan cheese

Salt and freshly ground black pepper

Steam the spinach for 1 minute. Squeeze any moisture from the spinach and place it in a blender or food processor with the parsley, basil, garlic, pine nuts, oil, Parmesan, and salt and pepper to taste. Blend until smooth.

**MAKES ABOUT 1 CUP**

Per 2 tablespoons: 84 calories, 8 g fat, 2 g protein, 2 g carbohydrates, 1 g fiber, 0 mg cholesterol, 67 mg sodium

**Variation:** Parmesan cheese may be substituted for the soy Parmesan.

# ARUGULA PESTO

*A blending of the East and West results in this assertive, creamy pesto that can transform spaghetti squash or other vegetable "pastas," as it does in the recipe for Carrot and Zucchini "Linguine" with Edamame, Black Olives, and Arugula Pesto (page 140). It is also delicious with whole grain dishes, roasted vegetables, baked tofu, or veggie burgers.*

  3 cloves garlic

  4 cups arugula

  3 tablespoons white miso

  1 tablespoon umeboshi vinegar

  ½ cup tahini paste

  ¼ cup olive oil

Chop the garlic in a food processor. Add the arugula and process until finely chopped. Add the miso, vinegar, and tahini and continue to process until combined. With the machine running, slowly stream in the oil and process until smooth and creamy.

**MAKES ABOUT 1¼ CUPS**

Per 2 tablespoons: 132 calories, 12 g fat, 3 g protein, 5 g carbohydrates, 1 g fiber, 0 mg cholesterol, 148 mg sodium

# SPICY PEANUT SAUCE

*Use this versatile sauce as a dipping sauce for spring rolls, roasted veggies, or baked tofu chunks. Or use it as a sauce over vegetable patties, veggie "pasta," or just about anything that needs a flavor infusion. For a mellow taste, omit the red-pepper flakes.*

½ cup creamy reduced-fat peanut butter

1 clove garlic, chopped

½ teaspoon finely chopped fresh ginger

½ teaspoon red-pepper flakes, or to taste

3 tablespoons low-sodium tamari soy sauce

2 tablespoons fresh lime juice

½ cup water

In a blender or food processor, blend the peanut butter, garlic, ginger, red-pepper flakes, tamari, lime juice, and water until smooth. Taste to adjust the seasoning. Use at once or cover and refrigerate until ready to use.

**MAKES ABOUT 1¼ CUPS**

Per 2 tablespoons: 80 calories, 7 g fat, 4 g protein, 3 g carbohydrates, 1 g fiber, 0 mg cholesterol, 241 mg sodium

# WILD MUSHROOM SAUCE

*Oozing with rich mushroom flavor, this sauce is terrific on roasted veggies, grain and bean dishes, veggie burgers, or baked tofu. Use it for dishes needing a rich brown sauce.*

1 ounce dried porcini or other wild mushrooms

1 tablespoon olive oil

2 shallots, finely chopped

2 cups chopped assorted fresh mushrooms (such as shiitake, oyster, porcini)

1½ cups vegetable stock

¼ cup white wine, red wine, or port

1 tablespoon low-sodium tamari soy sauce

Salt and freshly ground black pepper

Gravy Master or other food browning liquid (optional)

Soak the dried mushrooms in enough boiling water to cover and let stand for 30 minutes to soften. Chop the mushrooms, reserving the soaking liquid.

Heat the oil in a medium saucepan over medium heat. Add the shallots, cover, and cook until soft, about 3 minutes. Add the fresh mushrooms and cook 2 minutes longer. Stir in the stock, wine or port, tamari, reserved mushrooms and their soaking liquid, and salt and pepper to taste. Bring to a boil, then reduce the heat to low; cook, stirring, until the liquid is reduced by half. Add a few drops of Gravy Master (if desired) for a richer color. Serve hot.

**MAKES ABOUT 2 CUPS**

Per ¼ cup: 48 calories, 2 g fat, 2 g protein, 4 g carbohydrates, 1 g fiber, 0 mg cholesterol, 164 mg sodium

# "BASIC BLACK" BEAN SAUCE

*A sauce that "goes with anything." It's especially good on veggie burgers or sautéed seitan, tempeh, or tofu. Also good on grain dishes. For a spicier version, add some finely chopped chile peppers when you sauté the garlic.*

2 teaspoons olive oil

2 cloves garlic, chopped

1 cup cooked black beans

1 teaspoon low-sodium tamari soy sauce

½ cup water

Heat the oil in a medium skillet over medium heat. Add the garlic and cook until fragrant, 30 seconds. Stir in the beans and tamari and cook for 3 to 4 minutes to allow the flavors to mingle. Transfer the mixture to a blender or food processor and blend in just enough water to make a smooth, creamy sauce. Transfer to a small saucepan and taste to adjust the seasoning. Stir over low heat until hot.

**MAKES ABOUT 1 CUP**

Per ¼ cup: 79 calories, 3 g fat, 4 g protein, 9 g carbohydrates, 4 g fiber, 0 mg cholesterol, 301 mg sodium

# CREAMY CASHEW SAUCE

*This dairy-free sauce is made with protein-rich nuts and soy. Use it as you would any creamy white sauce. It's an integral part of Summer Squash "Paglia e Fieno" with Creamy Cashew Sauce (page 153). For a garlicky sauce, substitute 2 cloves of garlic for the onion. To give it a flavor similar to an Alfredo sauce, add some Parmesan cheese at serving time.*

1 tablespoon olive oil

3 tablespoons finely chopped sweet yellow onion

2 tablespoons dry white wine

¼ cup raw cashews

1½ cups vegetable stock

½ cup soft tofu

Pinch of ground nutmeg

Salt and freshly ground white pepper

Heat the oil in a small skillet over medium-low heat. Add the onion and cook until soft, about 2 minutes. Do not brown. Stir in the wine and set aside.

Using a blender, grind the cashews to a powder. Add half of the stock and blend until smooth. Add the remaining stock and the tofu and process until blended. Add the reserved onion mixture and process until thoroughly smooth. Transfer the sauce to a small saucepan and heat over low heat. Season with nutmeg and salt and pepper to taste. Serve warm.

**MAKES ABOUT 2 CUPS**

Per ¼ cup: 59 calories, 4 g fat, 2 g protein, 3 g carbohydrates, 1 g fiber, 0 mg cholesterol, 113 mg sodium

# SAUCE OF FOUR MUSTARDS

*Mustard lovers will want to use this as a sauce for veggie burgers, grains, or slaw or as a dipping sauce for lightly steamed vegetables or baked tofu chunks.*

- ½ cup soft tofu, well drained
- 1 tablespoon olive oil
- 1 tablespoon coarse-grained mustard
- 1 tablespoon Dijon mustard
- 1 tablespoon prepared yellow mustard
- 1 teaspoon fresh lemon juice
- ½ teaspoon mustard powder
- 1 tablespoon finely chopped fresh flat-leaf parsley
- 1 tablespoon finely chopped scallion or chives
- ½ teaspoon salt
- ⅛ teaspoon freshly ground black pepper

In a blender or food processor, combine the tofu, oil, coarse mustard, Dijon mustard, yellow mustard, lemon juice, mustard powder, parsley, scallion or chives, salt, and pepper. Blend until smooth.

**MAKES ABOUT ¾ CUP**

Per ¼ cup: 45 calories, 2 g fat, 3 g protein, 2 g carbohydrates, 0 g fiber, 0 mg cholesterol, 752 mg sodium

# RED PEPPER COULIS

*Intensely colored, this rich red pepper puree is simple to make and extremely low in carbohydrates. It can add a sophisticated nuance to a simple meal—spoon the coulis under a stack of roasted vegetables or stuffed zucchini, for instance.*

- 1 tablespoon olive oil
- 2 large red bell peppers, chopped
- 2 tablespoons finely chopped onion
- 2 tablespoons water
- Salt and freshly ground black pepper

Heat the oil in a large skillet over medium heat. Add the bell peppers and onion. Cover and cook for 5 minutes, to soften. Stir in the water and salt and black pepper to taste. Cover and cook until the vegetables are very soft, about 10 minutes. Transfer the vegetables to a food processor and blend until smooth. Use a fine-mesh strainer to strain the mixture into a saucepan. Keep warm over low heat until ready to use.

**MAKES ABOUT 1 CUP**

Per ¼ cup: 54 calories, 3 g fat, 1 g protein, 6 g carbohydrates, 2 g fiber, 0 mg cholesterol, 63 mg sodium

## LESS IS MORE

It takes just a small amount of high-fat foods—such as avocado, coconut, and nuts—to add big flavor to dishes. In other words, a little goes a long way. The same is true for potent ingredients such as alcoholic beverages: A mere splash of wine can add loads of flavor to a recipe.

# HOT-AS-HADES HARISSA SAUCE

*This super-hot Tunisian sauce is available in Middle Eastern markets; however, when you make your own, you can control the heat. In addition to the chile peppers and the olive oil, heady spices such as caraway and coriander make this a flavor explosion.*

⅓ cup dried hot red chile peppers, seeded and cut into small pieces

2 teaspoons caraway seeds

1 tablespoon coriander seeds

1 teaspoon cumin seeds

2 roasted red bell peppers (see note)

3 cloves garlic, chopped

½ teaspoon salt

3 tablespoons extra virgin olive oil

¼ cup water

Cover the chile peppers with boiling water in a heatproof bowl and soak for 30 minutes.

In a small skillet, stir the caraway, coriander, and cumin seeds over low heat until fragrant, about 30 seconds. Transfer to a food processor and add the soaked chile peppers, roasted bell peppers, garlic, and salt. Grind to a paste. Add the oil and water and blend to a smooth paste.

**MAKES ABOUT 1½ CUPS**

Per ¼ cup: 85 calories, 7 g fat, 1 g protein, 5 g carbohydrates, 2 g fiber, 0 mg cholesterol, 193 mg sodium

Note: Roast bell peppers by holding them directly over a gas flame with a pair of tongs until the skin blackens on all sides. (They can also be roasted under a broiler, turning until the skin blackens all over.) Place the blackened peppers in a paper bag and set them aside for 10 minutes, or until cool enough to touch with your hands. Remove the blackened skin and the seeds and proceed with the recipe. If you'd rather not roast your own peppers, you can purchase jars of roasted red bell peppers in supermarkets.

# SULTRY SUMMER SALSA

*Store-bought salsa pales in comparison with the bright, fresh flavors of this homemade version. It's an especially colorful salsa made with yellow bell pepper and plum tomatoes against a backdrop of green. The sweetness of the yellow pepper complements the lime, cilantro, and jalapeño pepper, while the tomatillos add just the right amount of tartness. Amp up the heat by adding more jalapeño peppers.*

2 tomatillos, husks removed

3 firm plum tomatoes, coarsely chopped

2 scallions, chopped

1 yellow bell pepper, finely chopped

1 jalapeño pepper or other small hot chile pepper, seeded and chopped

2 tablespoons finely chopped onion

Juice of 1 lime

2 tablespoons finely chopped fresh cilantro

2 tablespoons finely chopped fresh flat-leaf parsley

Salt and freshly ground black pepper

Cook the tomatillos in a small saucepan of boiling water until just tender, about 5 minutes. Drain, coarsely chop, and place in a large bowl. Add the tomatoes, scallions, bell pepper, jalapeño pepper, onion, lime juice, cilantro, parsley, and salt and pepper to taste. Mix to combine. Cover and let stand at room temperature for 1 hour before serving. If not using right away, store in the refrigerator. The salsa will keep refrigerated for 3 to 4 days.

**MAKES ABOUT 2 CUPS**

Per ¼ cup: 22 calories, 0 g fat, 1 g protein, 5 g carbohydrates, 2 g fiber, 0 mg cholesterol, 5 mg sodium

# CHARMOULA SAUCE

*Perfectly paired with the portobello patties on page 136, this flavorful sauce is also delicious with baked tofu. Just slather the tofu with the sauce and bake for 30 minutes at 375°F.*

- ¼ cup chopped fresh flat-leaf parsley
- ¼ cup chopped fresh cilantro
- ¼ cup olive oil
- 2 cloves garlic, finely chopped
- 2½ tablespoons fresh lemon juice
- ½ teaspoon ground paprika
- ½ teaspoon salt
- ¼ teaspoon ground red pepper
- ¼ teaspoon ground cumin
- ¼ teaspoon ground ginger

In a blender or food processor, combine the parsley, cilantro, oil, garlic, lemon juice, paprika, salt, ground red pepper, cumin, and ginger. Blend until smooth.

**MAKES ABOUT 1 CUP**

Per ¼ cup: 128 calories, 14 g fat, 0 g protein, 2 g carbohydrates, 0 g fiber, 0 mg cholesterol, 294 mg sodium

# HEART-HEALTHY HOLLANDAISE

*Now you can enjoy a lemony hollandaise-like sauce that uses no eggs or butter. Made with soy and olive oil, this version is much better for your heart and is a great sauce for Tofu Benedict (pages 182–183) or roasted asparagus. If you use soy sour cream, Tofutti is a good brand.*

¾ cup soft tofu or soy sour cream

¼ cup soy milk

1½ tablespoons fresh lemon juice

1 tablespoon olive oil

½ teaspoon salt (if using tofu)

Pinch of ground turmeric

Pinch of ground paprika

Pinch of ground red pepper

In a food processor or blender, combine the tofu or sour cream, milk, lemon juice, oil, salt (if using), turmeric, paprika, and ground red pepper. Blend until smooth.

## MAKES ABOUT 1 CUP

Per ¼ cup: 65 calories, 5 g fat, 3 g protein, 2 g carbohydrates, 0 g fiber, 0 mg cholesterol, 296 mg sodium

**Variation:** Cow's milk may be substituted for the soy milk.

# GODDESS-INSPIRED DRESSING

*I drew inspiration from classic green goddess dressing, a mayonnaise-and-anchovy concoction famous from the 1920s. This version retains the fresh green herbs of the original—with virtuous tofu replacing the eggy mayonnaise and piquant capers standing in for the salty anchovies.*

½ cup chopped fresh flat-leaf parsley

½ cup tofu, well drained (see note)

2 scallions, finely chopped

1 tablespoon finely chopped fresh tarragon or 1 teaspoon dried tarragon

2 teaspoons capers, rinsed and drained

1 clove garlic, crushed

3 tablespoons tarragon vinegar or cider vinegar

2 tablespoons extra virgin olive oil

½ teaspoon salt

¼ teaspoon freshly ground black pepper

In a blender or food processor, combine the parsley, tofu, scallions, tarragon, capers, garlic, vinegar, oil, salt, and pepper. Blend until smooth, scraping down the sides of the container as needed. Add a little water if the dressing is too thick. Taste to adjust the seasoning. Transfer to a container and refrigerate, covered, until ready to serve.

**MAKES ABOUT 1 CUP**

Per 2 tablespoons: 48 calories, 4 g fat, 1 g protein, 2 g carbohydrates, 1 g fiber, 0 mg cholesterol, 215 mg sodium

Note: A soy-based mayonnaise, such as Vegenaise or Nayonaise, may be used instead of the tofu.

## SHALLOT AND SUN-DRIED TOMATO VINAIGRETTE WITH PINE NUTS

*The sun-dried tomato gives this light and luscious dressing rich depth of flavor. It tastes great on any green salad.*

2 shallots, chopped

1 sun-dried tomato, soaked and chopped

2 tablespoons pine nuts

¼ teaspoon salt

3 tablespoons balsamic vinegar

½ cup extra virgin olive oil

Freshly ground black pepper

In a blender or food processor, combine the shallots, tomato, pine nuts, and salt; blend well. Add the vinegar, oil, and pepper to taste and process until smooth.

**MAKES ABOUT ¾ CUP**

**Per 2 tablespoons: 183 calories, 19 g fat, 1 g protein, 2 g carbohydrates, 0 g fiber, 0 mg cholesterol, 106 mg sodium**

# SESAME-GINGER DRESSING

*If smooth, creamy, and loaded with flavor weren't enough to ask from a salad dressing, this one also provides protein and calcium, thanks to the tofu and tahini.*

¼ cup soft tofu, well drained

1 tablespoon tahini paste

1 tablespoon finely chopped fresh ginger

1 tablespoon finely chopped scallion

2 tablespoons fresh lemon juice

1 tablespoon low-sodium tamari soy sauce

1 tablespoon rice vinegar

2 tablespoons toasted sesame oil

In a blender or food processor, combine the tofu, tahini, ginger, scallion, lemon juice, tamari, vinegar, and oil. Blend until smooth, scraping down the sides of the container as needed.

**MAKES ABOUT ¾ CUP**

Per 2 tablespoons: 65 calories, 6 g fat, 1 g protein, 2 g carbohydrates, 0 g fiber, 0 mg cholesterol, 103 mg sodium

# CREAMY CUCUMBER-DIJON DRESSING

*The fresh dill complements the crisp, clean flavor of the cucumber in this light and creamy salad dressing.*

    1 cucumber, peeled, seeded, and chopped
    1 shallot, chopped
    ¼ cup soft tofu
    1 tablespoon olive oil
    1 tablespoon fresh lemon juice
    1 tablespoon chopped fresh dill
    2 teaspoons Dijon mustard
    ¼ teaspoon salt

In a blender or food processor, combine the cucumber, shallot, tofu, oil, lemon juice, dill, mustard, and salt. Blend until smooth, scraping down the sides of the container as needed.

**MAKES ABOUT ¾ CUP**

Per 2 tablespoons: 36 calories, 3 g fat, 1 g protein, 2 g carbohydrates, 0 g fiber, 0 mg cholesterol, 141 mg sodium

**Variation:** Substitute sour cream or yogurt for the tofu.

# WHITE WINE VINEGAR AND FRESH HERB MARINADE

*Employ this flavorful marinade when grilled vegetables are on the menu.*

¼ cup white wine vinegar

¼ cup olive oil

1 clove garlic, crushed

2 tablespoons finely chopped fresh basil

1 tablespoon finely chopped fresh savory

1 teaspoon finely chopped fresh thyme

1 teaspoon finely chopped fresh marjoram

In a small bowl, combine the vinegar, oil, and garlic. Whisk to blend. Stir in the basil, savory, thyme, and marjoram. Cover and refrigerate until ready to use.

**MAKES ABOUT ½ CUP**

Per 2 tablespoons: 128 calories, 14 g fat, 0 g protein, 2 g carbohydrates, 0 g fiber, 0 mg cholesterol, 77 mg sodium

# CHAPTER EIGHT

# BREAKFAST BITES

From fruit smoothies to cereals to bagels, many vegetarian breakfasts are high in carbohydrates. When I became vegetarian, I was so pleased to get away from the high-cholesterol bacon and eggs breakfasts that I didn't realize the extra-large white-flour bagel I enjoyed each morning would begin to take its toll in added pounds. Still, there are lots of delicious and nourishing ways to enjoy the first meal of the day.

One quick and easy choice is to keep frozen veggie bacon, sausage links, or patties on hand. They can be eaten alone or with scrambled tofu for a low-carb, protein-rich, cholesterol-free breakfast. Tofu makes a versatile egg substitute, as shown in the recipes in this chapter for Spinach-Mushroom "Frittata," Scrambled Tofu with Peperonata, and Tofu Benedict.

Even pancakes aren't out of the question when made with whole grain oats and omega-rich flax. And smoothies can still be reasonably low carb—especially when you use fruit on the lower end of the glycemic index, such as berries (see pages 190–191). Use a little natural sweetener and add some tofu, flax, or soy protein powder for an extra boost, if you like. They are all great ways to start your day.

# SPINACH-MUSHROOM "FRITTATA"

*Ideal for brunch, lunch, or a light supper, this egg-free "frittata" is satisfying and delicious.*

2 tablespoons olive oil

½ cup finely chopped onion

1 cup sliced white mushrooms

1 cup cooked chopped fresh or frozen spinach, squeezed dry

1 pound firm tofu, squeezed and patted dry

⅛ teaspoon ground turmeric

½ teaspoon salt

⅛ teaspoon freshly ground black pepper

½ cup shredded soy mozzarella cheese

Preheat the oven to 375°F.

Heat 1 tablespoon of the oil in a large skillet over medium heat. Add the onion, cover, and cook until softened, about 3 minutes. Add the mushrooms and cook, stirring occasionally, until the liquid is released from the mushrooms. Continue cooking until the liquid is absorbed. Stir in the spinach and cook a minute longer. Spoon the vegetable mixture into a lightly oiled shallow round baking dish and set aside.

In a food processor, combine the tofu, turmeric, salt, and pepper and process until smooth. Pour over the vegetables and add the mozzarella, mixing gently to combine. Bake until firm and golden brown on top, about 25 minutes. Let cool for a few minutes before cutting into wedges to serve.

**SERVES 4**

Per serving: 203 calories, 13 g fat, 16 g protein, 10 g carbohydrates, 2 g fiber, 0 mg cholesterol, 591 mg sodium

**Variation:** Use regular mozzarella cheese instead of the soy cheese.

# VERY VEGGIE HASH

*This is a great way to use up leftover vegetables and other ingredients to make a satisfying and tasty meal.*

- 1 tablespoon olive oil
- 1 small yellow onion, chopped
- 1 red or yellow bell pepper, chopped
- 8 ounces white mushrooms, coarsely chopped
- 2 frozen vegetarian burgers, thawed and chopped (see note)
- 3 cups chopped cooked cauliflower
- 1 cup chopped cooked Brussels sprouts (see note)
- 1 tablespoon low-sodium tamari soy sauce
- Salt and freshly ground black pepper

Heat the oil in a large skillet over medium heat. Add the onion, cover, and cook until tender, about 5 minutes. Add the bell pepper and mushrooms and cook until tender, about 5 minutes. Add the burgers, cauliflower, Brussels sprouts, tamari, and salt and pepper to taste. Cook until heated through, about 5 minutes longer.

## SERVES 4

Per serving: 166 calories, 6 g fat, 12 g protein, 20 g carbohydrates, 9 g fiber, 0 mg cholesterol, 339 mg sodium

Note: You may replace the burgers with 1½ cups frozen vegetarian burger crumbles, thawed. You may replace the Brussels sprouts with zucchini or another cooked vegetable you have on hand.

# TOFU BENEDICT

*This recipe works best using a nonstick skillet. If you don't have one, you may bake the tofu in an oiled baking pan at 375°F for 20 minutes. Yves brand is a good choice for the vegetarian Canadian bacon.*

**4 very thin slices tomato**

**4 slices vegetarian Canadian bacon**

**1 pound extra-firm tofu**

**1 tablespoon olive oil**

**Salt and freshly ground black pepper**

**Pinch of ground turmeric**

**Pinch of ground paprika**

**2 whole grain or low-carb English muffins or crumpets, split**

**1 cup Heart-Healthy Hollandaise (page 172)**

**Finely chopped fresh flat-leaf parsley**

Preheat the oven to 300°F. Arrange the tomato slices and bacon slices on a lightly oiled baking sheet and place in the oven while you prepare the tofu.

Cut the tofu horizontally into 4 slabs. Using a 4-inch round cutter or a knife, cut each slab into a piece the size of an English muffin half. (Use the leftover scraps of tofu in another recipe.) Rub the tofu rounds with ½ tablespoon oil and season with salt, pepper, turmeric, and paprika to taste, rubbing in the spices to color the tofu.

Heat the remaining ½ tablespoon oil in a large nonstick skillet over medium heat. Add the tofu and cook until hot and golden brown on both sides, turning once, about 10 minutes total.

Remove the tomato and bacon slices from the oven. Top each bacon slice with a tofu round and then place a tomato slice on top of each tofu round. Reduce the oven temperature to 200°F and place the baking sheet back into the oven.

Toast the English muffins or crumpets in a toaster. Warm the hollandaise sauce in a small saucepan over low heat until just warm, being careful not to boil it. To serve, arrange the muffin or crumpet halves on plates, cut side up; top each with a bacon stack and spoon some hollandaise sauce on top of each. Garnish with the parsley. Serve at once.

**SERVES 4**

Per serving: 268 calories, 16 g fat, 21 g protein, 12 g carbohydrates, 1 g fiber, 0 mg cholesterol, 939 mg sodium

# SCRAMBLED TOFU WITH PEPERONATA

*The Italian stewed pepper dish called peperonata tastes better after it sits awhile, so if you plan to jazz up your morning tofu scramble, make the peperonata the day before.*

2 tablespoons olive oil

½ cup finely chopped onion

1 red bell pepper, chopped

1 green bell pepper, chopped

2 cloves garlic, finely chopped

1 can (14½ ounces) chopped tomatoes, drained

Salt and freshly ground black pepper

2 scallions, finely chopped

1 pound firm tofu, drained well and crumbled

Pinch of ground turmeric

Finely chopped fresh flat-leaf parsley or basil

Heat 1 tablespoon of the oil in a medium saucepan over medium heat. Add the onion, cover, and cook until softened, about 2 minutes. Add the bell peppers and garlic and cook 5 minutes to soften. Stir in the tomatoes and salt and pepper to taste. Reduce the heat to low and cook, covered, until the peppers are soft, about 10 minutes. Set aside, but keep warm.

Heat the remaining 1 tablespoon oil in a large skillet over medium heat. Add the scallions, tofu, and turmeric. Season with salt and pepper to taste and cook, stirring, until the tofu is hot and the liquid is absorbed, 8 to 10 minutes. To serve, divide the tofu among individual plates and top with the peperonata and parsley or basil.

### SERVES 4

Per serving: 103 calories, 11 g fat, 9 g protein, 16 g carbohydrates, 4 g fiber, 0 mg cholesterol, 25 mg sodium

# SOY-GOOD BREAKFAST CASSEROLE

*Now a hearty breakfast can be convenient, too! Assemble this casserole the night before and pop it into the oven in the morning. For an even quicker breakfast, bake it ahead of time as well and then just warm it in the oven or microwave when it's time to eat.*

1 tablespoon olive oil

¼ cup chopped onion

½ cup chopped bell pepper (any color)

8 ounces white mushrooms, chopped

8 ounces vegetarian sausage, chopped

1 cup cooked spinach, drained, squeezed dry, and chopped

1 package (16 ounces) firm tofu, drained

½ cup shredded soy mozzarella cheese

½ teaspoon salt

⅛ teaspoon freshly ground black pepper

Preheat the oven to 375°F. Coat a shallow 2-quart baking dish with cooking spray.

Heat the oil in a large skillet over medium heat. Add the onion and pepper, cover, and cook until softened, 5 minutes. Stir in the mushrooms and cook until tender, 5 minutes. Add the sausage and spinach and stir to combine. Transfer the mixture to the prepared dish and set aside.

In a food processor, combine the tofu, mozzarella, salt, and pepper. Process until smooth. Spread the tofu mixture over the mixture in the baking dish. Bake until firm and lightly browned on top, 20 to 30 minutes.

### SERVES 4

Per serving: 311 calories, 20 g fat, 24 g protein, 14 g carbohydrates, 4 g fiber, 0 mg cholesterol, 918 mg sodium

**Variation:** Substitute regular mozzarella cheese for the soy mozzarella.

# APPLES AND OATS FLAXJACKS

*It's almost like having apple pie for breakfast! Everyone will love these, and no one will suspect how healthy they are. Flaxseeds are an important source of omega-3 essential fatty acids. In this recipe, ground flaxseeds blended with water replace the standard eggs.*

1½ cups old-fashioned rolled oats

2 teaspoons baking powder

½ teaspoon ground cinnamon

½ teaspoon salt

2 tablespoons ground flaxseeds

¼ cup water

1¼ cups soy milk or other dairy-free milk

1 tablespoon agave syrup or ¼ teaspoon stevia

1 teaspoon vanilla extract

1 large Granny Smith or other baking apple, peeled, cored, and shredded

Preheat the oven to 200°F.

In a blender, grind the oats to a fine powder and transfer to a large bowl. Add the baking powder, cinnamon, and salt and set aside.

In the blender, combine the flaxseeds and water and blend until thick, about 30 seconds. Add the milk, agave syrup or stevia, and vanilla and blend until smooth. Pour into the oat mixture and combine with a few swift strokes until just moistened. Fold in the apple.

Ladle scant ¼ cupfuls of the batter onto a hot, lightly oiled griddle or nonstick skillet. Cook until small bubbles appear on the top of the pancakes, about 2 minutes. Flip the pancakes with a spatula and cook until the second side is lightly browned, about 1 minute longer. Repeat with the remaining batter, keeping the cooked pancakes warm in the oven.

## SERVES 6

Per serving: 126 calories, 3 g fat, 5 g protein, 20 g carbohydrates, 5 g fiber, 0 mg cholesterol, 364 mg sodium

**Variation:** Cow's milk may be substituted for the dairy-free milk.

# AWESOME OATMEAL

*Oatmeal made with old-fashioned rolled oats is an example of whole grain "good" carbs that should be an important part of your diet. In this recipe, ground flaxseeds—with their beneficial omega-3s—give the oatmeal an extra boost of nutrition. Add agave syrup if you want a little sweetener.*

> 3 cups water
> 1½ cups old-fashioned rolled oats
> ½ teaspoon ground cinnamon
> Pinch of salt
> 2 tablespoons ground flaxseeds
> 1 tablespoon agave syrup (optional)

Bring the water to a boil in a medium saucepan over high heat. Stir in the oats, cinnamon, and salt. Reduce the heat to low, cover, and simmer for 5 minutes, stirring occasionally. Remove from the heat. Cover and let stand for 2 minutes. To serve, spoon the oatmeal into bowls and sprinkle with the flaxseeds and agave syrup (if using).

**SERVES 4**

Per serving: 153 calories, 4 g fat, 6 g protein, 23 g carbohydrates, 5 g fiber, 0 mg cholesterol, 6 mg sodium

## FLAX FACTS

Flax is rich in essential omega-3 fatty acids, so it should be an integral part of your daily diet. That's easy to accomplish. Add a tablespoon of ground flaxseeds to your smoothie or oatmeal at breakfast. Sprinkle some on your salad or veggies at lunch or dinner. If you prefer, you can use flaxseed oil instead of the seeds—just remember that this oil should not be heated, so use it on salads. Both flaxseeds and the oil are highly perishable and go rancid quickly. Store them in airtight containers in the refrigerator.

# MOCHA CABANA

*Coffee and chocolate lovers will enjoy this delicious blender drink. Freezing the coffee into ice cubes helps to thicken the drink, so plan ahead and freeze your coffee the day before or keep some "coffee cubes" on hand for convenience.*

1½ cups chilled soy milk

2 tablespoons unsweetened cocoa powder

1 tablespoon agave syrup or ⅛ teaspoon stevia, or to taste

1¼ cups strong brewed coffee, frozen into ice cubes

1 teaspoon vanilla extract

In a blender, combine the milk, cocoa powder, agave syrup or stevia, coffee, and vanilla. Blend until thick and smooth.

### SERVES 1

Per serving: 166 calories, 9 g fat, 13 g protein, 15 g carbohydrates, 8 g fiber, 0 mg cholesterol, 53 mg sodium

**Variation:** Substitute milk for the soy milk.

## PURPLE PASSION SMOOTHIE

*This is a great way to enjoy fresh berries in season or frozen berries the rest of the time. It's so thick and creamy you'll want to eat it with a spoon. The frozen banana adds creaminess as well as potassium and other nutrients.*

1½ cups fresh or frozen blueberries

½ cup soy milk

½ banana, peeled, cut into chunks, and frozen

6 ice cubes

In a blender, combine the blueberries, milk, banana, and ice cubes and blend until smooth.

**SERVES 2**

Per serving: 109 calories, 2 g fat, 3 g protein, 24 g carbohydrates, 5 g fiber, 0 mg cholesterol, 14 mg sodium

**Variation:** Substitute milk for the soy milk.

## SOY SMART SMOOTHIES

Smoothies are a great way to add beneficial soy to your diet. Just add soy milk, tofu, or a scoop of soy protein powder to your favorite fruit smoothie.

# SENSATIONAL STRAWBERRY SMOOTHIE

*If your strawberries are less than perfectly sweet, you may need to add a small amount of agave syrup, stevia, or other natural low-carb sweetener.*

1½ cups fresh or frozen strawberries

½ cup soft tofu

½ cup natural fruit-sweetened cranberry juice

1 teaspoon vanilla extract

6 ice cubes

Combine the strawberries, tofu, juice, vanilla, and ice cubes in a blender and blend until smooth, adding a little more juice if needed for the desired consistency.

**SERVES 2**

Per serving: 108 calories, 3 g fat, 5 g protein, 17 g carbohydrates, 3 g fiber, 0 mg cholesterol, 11 mg sodium

## TOAST OF THE TOWN

For a quick and nourishing breakfast, toast a slice of whole grain, sprouted, or flourless bread (sprouted whole grain Ezekiel bread is a good choice). Spread it with almond butter and sprinkle on some ground flaxseeds.

# CHAPTER NINE

# DIVINE DESSERTS

Where bad carbohydrates are concerned, desserts usually hit the jackpot. Most contain white flour and white sugar, and many are also loaded with saturated fat and cholesterol. But what fun is life without dessert? The solution is to choose ingredients that maximize nutrition and minimize empty carbs and saturated fat.

The recipes in this chapter fit the bill by focusing on desserts made with fruits, nuts, and even chocolate. For sweetener, I prefer to use agave syrup or stevia. (For more information about sweeteners, see chapter one.) These desserts are definitely not *no* carb, but as desserts go, they're certainly moderate in carbohydrates and made with healthful ingredients. So you should be able to enjoy an occasional dessert even when trying to eat healthy or to lose weight.

# TWO-BERRY PIE WITH PECAN-SUNFLOWER CRUST

*This nutty, protein-packed crust filled with sweet fresh-from-the-field berries is a perfect blending of great taste and good-for-you nutrition. This pie is especially yummy topped with the cashew creme from Peach-Blueberry Parfaits with Cashew Creme (page 202). For a sweeter crust, substitute dates for the dried plums—but be forewarned: Dates are higher in carbs. Psyllium, a natural fiber available in powdered form in natural food stores, is used here as a thickening agent.*

1½ cups pecan pieces

½ cup unsalted sunflower seeds

¼ cup pitted dried plums (prunes)

¼ teaspoon stevia, or to taste

2 cups blueberries

2 cups sliced strawberries

2 teaspoons fresh lemon juice

2 teaspoons psyllium powder

Place the pecans and sunflower seeds in a food processor and process until coarsely ground. Add the dried plums, 1 teaspoon psyllium, and ⅛ teaspoon stevia; process until thoroughly combined. Press the mixture into a 9-inch pie plate.

Combine the blueberries and 1½ cups strawberries. Place in the crust and set aside.

In a food processor, combine the remaining ½ cup strawberries, lemon juice, the remaining 1 teaspoon psyllium, and the remaining ⅛ teaspoon stevia. Blend until smooth. Taste to adjust sweetness. Pour the sauce mixture over the berries and refrigerate for 1 hour before serving. For best results, serve this pie the same day that it is made.

## SERVES 8

Per serving: 261 calories, 21 g fat, 5 g protein, 17 g carbohydrates, 6 g fiber, 0 mg cholesterol, 12 mg sodium

# CHOCOLATE SILK PIE

*This creamy, chocolatey pie tastes so yummy you may forget it's low carb and cholesterol free. For a sweeter (albeit higher-carb) crust, substitute pitted dates for the dried plums.*

- 1½ cups blanched almonds
- ⅓ cup pitted dried plums (prunes)
- 1 package (12 ounces) extra-firm silken tofu, well drained
- ¼ teaspoon stevia
- 2 tablespoons unsweetened cocoa powder
- 1½ teaspoons vanilla extract

Finely grind the almonds in a food processor, then add the dried plums and blend until combined. Press the mixture into a 9-inch pie plate and set aside.

In a food processor, combine the tofu, stevia, cocoa powder, and vanilla and blend until smooth. Pour the filling mixture into the prepared crust and refrigerate for at least 2 hours before serving.

**SERVES 6**

Per serving: 207 calories, 14 g fat, 9 g protein, 13 g carbohydrates, 4 g fiber, 0 mg cholesterol, 21 mg sodium

# BLUEBERRY CHEESECAKE WITH GRANOLA CRUST

*Blueberries are low in carbs and rich in beneficial phytochemicals. When very ripe, they are sweet enough to enjoy without added sugar. The cream cheese and the silken tofu provide a protein-rich, cholesterol-free base for this updated version of classic cheesecake. Look for low-carb granola at supermarkets and natural food stores. For best results, have the ingredients at room temperature before starting.*

1½ cups granola (preferably low carb)

¼ cup nonhydrogenated, trans-free margarine, melted

2 containers (8 ounces each) tofu cream cheese

8 ounces firm regular or silken tofu

½ teaspoon stevia, or to taste

1 teaspoon vanilla extract

2 tablespoons fruit-sweetened blueberry spread

1 tablespoon water

2–3 cups blueberries

Preheat the oven to 350°F.

In a food processor, combine the granola and margarine until well blended. Press the crust mixture into the bottom and halfway up the sides of a 9" springform pan that has been lightly coated with cooking spray. Set aside.

In a food processor, combine the cream cheese and tofu; blend well. Add the stevia and vanilla and blend until smooth. Pour the filling into the prepared crust.

Bake until firm, about 40 minutes. Turn the oven off and leave the cheesecake inside for 30 minutes. Remove the cake from the oven and cool to room temperature, then chill for several hours in the refrigerator.

While the cake is chilling, make the topping. Combine the blueberry spread and water in a small saucepan and stir over low heat until smooth. Add the blueberries and cook until slightly softened and coated with the spread. Taste for sweetness and add a little sweetener if necessary. Set aside to cool.

Once the cake is chilled, remove the sides of the pan and spoon the topping evenly over the top of the cheesecake.

**SERVES 8**

Per serving: 389 calories, 31 g fat, 7 g protein, 22 g carbohydrates, 3 g fiber, 0 mg cholesterol, 359 mg sodium

**Variation:** Substitute butter for the margarine and use regular cream cheese instead of tofu cream cheese.

## HOW LOW CAN YOU GO?

It's time for a low-carb reality check. Some extremely low-carb diets recommend consuming between 10 and 20 grams of carbohydrates per day; others suggest less than 50 grams per day. At the other end of the spectrum, a high-carb diet would be one in which you consume over 250 grams of carbs each day.

What should you aim for? According to recent nutritional guidelines, 130 grams of carbohydrates is the minimum amount per day needed for good health. For a commonsense approach to dieting, try to stay around that amount, making sure those carbs are high-quality, nutritious whole foods. Combine this with a sensible exercise plan. As always, before beginning any weight loss program, be sure to consult a health care practitioner.

# CRUSTLESS APPLE CRUMB PIE

*Fresh out of the oven, this looks and smells like an apple crumb pie. But without the refined carbs found in a typical crust, this version is much better for you. It is delicious served warm, but it will cut into wedges better once cooled.*

**5 Granny Smith apples, peeled, cored, and sliced**

**¼ teaspoon stevia or 2 tablespoons agave syrup**

**1 tablespoon fresh lemon juice**

**1½ teaspoons ground cinnamon**

**1¼ cups rolled oats**

**3 tablespoons nonhydrogenated, trans-free margarine, softened**

Preheat the oven to 375°F. Lightly oil a 10" pie plate and set aside.

In a large bowl, combine the apples, half of the stevia or agave syrup, lemon juice, and 1 teaspoon of the cinnamon. Mix gently and transfer to the prepared dish; set aside.

In a small bowl, combine the oats, the remaining ½ teaspoon cinnamon, the remaining stevia or agave syrup, and the margarine. Mix with your hands to thoroughly combine. Sprinkle the topping over the apple mixture. Bake until the fruit is cooked and the topping is browned, 45 to 50 minutes.

**SERVES 8**

Per serving: 100 calories, 1 g fat, 2 g protein, 23 g carbohydrates, 4 g fiber, 0 mg cholesterol, 1 mg sodium

**Variation:** Substitute butter for the margarine.

# WALNUT AND CURRANT-STUFFED BAKED APPLES

*This comforting dessert is a great way to warm up on a chilly day.*

4 Granny Smith or other firm baking apples, cored
Juice of 1 lemon
½ cup finely chopped walnuts
2 tablespoons dried currants
1 tablespoon nonhydrogenated, trans-free margarine
2 tablespoons agave syrup
1 teaspoon ground cinnamon
1 cup water

Preheat the oven to 350°F.

Peel the top third of each apple. Rub the exposed flesh with the lemon juice to avoid discoloration.

In a small bowl, combine the walnuts, currants, margarine, 1 tablespoon agave syrup, and cinnamon; mix well. Stuff the mixture into the center of the apples and place them upright in a shallow casserole dish. Pour the water and the remaining 1 tablespoon agave syrup around the apples.

Bake until tender, about 1 hour. Serve warm.

**SERVES 4**

Per serving: 209 calories, 11 g fat, 2 g protein, 29 g carbohydrates, 7 g fiber, 0 mg cholesterol, 32 mg sodium

**Variation:** Substitute butter for the margarine.

# PECAN-STUDDED APPLE–ZUCCHINI CAKE

*Filled with good things from A to Z, this moist cake has just enough sweetness to satisfy those dessert cravings but is amazingly low in carbs. Because the apples and zucchini make this cake extremely moist, a dry sweetener should be used to avoid adding more liquid to the batter. A firm baking apple, such as Granny Smith, is best for this recipe.*

½ cup blanched almonds

½ cup whole wheat flour

½ cup soy flour or oat flour

1 tablespoon baking powder

½ teaspoon baking soda

1½ teaspoons ground cinnamon

½ teaspoon ground ginger

¼ teaspoon ground allspice

¼ teaspoon salt

1 teaspoon stevia

1 cup chopped pecans

¾ cup soy milk

2 cups shredded zucchini

1 apple, peeled, cored, and shredded

Preheat the oven to 350°F. Coat an 8" × 8" baking pan with cooking spray.

Finely grind the almonds in a food processor and place them in a mixing bowl. Stir in the whole wheat flour, soy or oat flour, baking powder, baking soda, cinnamon, ginger, allspice, salt, and stevia; mix well. Stir in the pecans, then stir in the soy milk, zucchini, and apple; mix until combined. Place the batter in the prepared pan.

Bake until the cake is browned on top and a tester comes out clean, about 45 minutes.

**SERVES 8**

Per serving: 160 calories, 12 g fat, 5 g protein, 10 g carbohydrates, 3 g fiber, 0 mg cholesterol, 302 mg sodium

**Variation:** Use dairy milk to replace the soy milk.

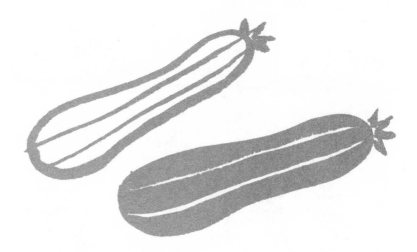

# PEACH-BLUEBERRY PARFAITS WITH CASHEW CREME

*Other fresh fruits—such as strawberries, raspberries, nectarines, or plums—may be used. Try to choose fruits on the lower end of the glycemic index (see page 224) and enjoy them when they're in season and at their peak of flavor so no added sweetener is necessary.*

1 cup cashews, toasted

½ cup water

1 package (12 ounces) silken tofu

1½ teaspoons vanilla extract

3 tablespoons plus 2 teaspoons agave syrup (see note)

3 peaches, peeled and sliced (about 2 cups)

1 teaspoon fresh lemon juice

2 cups blueberries

½ teaspoon ground cinnamon

Mint leaves

Grind the cashews to a powder in a blender. Add the water and blend until smooth. Add the tofu, vanilla, and 3 tablespoons agave syrup; blend until smooth and creamy. Transfer to a small bowl, cover, and refrigerate for 30 minutes.

In a medium bowl, mix the peaches, lemon juice, and 1 teaspoon agave syrup. In a separate bowl, mix the blueberries, cinnamon, and the remaining 1 teaspoon agave syrup.

Alternately spoon the blueberries, cashew creme, and peaches into parfait glasses, ending with a dollop of cashew creme. Garnish with mint leaves.

## SERVES 8

Per serving: 163 calories, 10 g fat, 6 g protein, 16 g carbohydrates, 2 g fiber, 0 mg cholesterol, 8 mg sodium

Note: You may replace the agave syrup with stevia. Blend ¼ teaspoon stevia with the tofu and cashew mixture. Add a healthy pinch of stevia to both the peaches and the blueberries.

# GRILLED FRUIT SKEWERS WITH STRAWBERRY COULIS

*For variety, use other lower-carb fruits, such as peaches, nectarines, and starfruit. If using bamboo skewers, be sure to soak them in water for 30 minutes to prevent burning.*

> 3 plums, halved, pitted, and cut into 1½" chunks
> ½ pineapple, peeled, cored, and cut into 1½" chunks
> 1 cup strawberries
> Fresh Strawberry Coulis (page 210)

Preheat the grill. Thread the fruit onto skewers in an alternating pattern. Grill on both sides just until grill marks start to appear, about 5 minutes per side. Arrange the skewered fruit on plates with small dipping bowls of the strawberry coulis.

**SERVES 4**

Per serving: 70 calories, 1 g fat, 1 g protein, 17 g carbohydrates, 2 g fiber, 0 mg cholesterol, 1 mg sodium

# VANILLA-SCENTED POACHED PEARS DIPPED IN CHOCOLATE

*This elegant dessert is a little fussy to prepare, but the results are well worth it for a special-occasion meal. Make sure the pears are just ripe, not too soft. I prefer Bosc pears for poaching because they have a firmer texture than other varieties.*

4 small Bosc pears

Juice of 1 lemon

1 tablespoon agave syrup or 1 teaspoon stevia

1¼ cups water

2 teaspoons vanilla extract

4 tablespoons nonhydrogenated, trans-free margarine

2 tablespoons semisweet chocolate chips

12 raspberries (optional)

4 mint sprigs (optional)

Peel, halve, and core the pears, leaving the stem intact. In a saucepan large enough to hold the pears in a single layer, combine the lemon juice, agave syrup or stevia, water, vanilla, and pears. Bring to a simmer, cover, and cook until the pears are tender, about 20 minutes.

Cool the pears and liquid together uncovered in the refrigerator. Once cool, remove the pears from the liquid and set aside.

Bring the liquid to a boil and cook until reduced by about three-quarters. Set the sauce aside.

In the top of a double boiler, combine the margarine and chocolate. Stir over barely simmering water until melted and smooth. Keep warm. Carefully dip each pear half into the chocolate.

Refrigerate the pear halves to allow the chocolate to cool. To serve, place the pears on dessert plates. Garnish with raspberries and mint leaves, if desired.

**SERVES 4**

Per serving: 234 calories, 14 g fat, 1 g protein, 28 g carbohydrates, 4 g fiber, 0 mg cholesterol, 116 mg sodium

**Variation:** Substitute butter for the margarine.

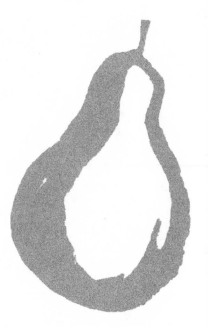

# CHOCOLATE–ALMOND BUTTER BALLS

*These tasty treats go together in a flash, look pretty, and have enough healthy ingredients that you could eat them for breakfast! For a festive occasion, consider adding a tablespoon of amaretto or other spirits to the mixture before rolling into balls.*

½ cup almond butter
1 cup wheat germ
¼ cup agave syrup
3 tablespoons unsweetened cocoa powder
½ cup ground toasted almonds

In a food processor, combine the almond butter, wheat germ, agave syrup, and cocoa; blend until well combined. Roll into 1" balls and set on a baking sheet. Roll in the ground nuts and refrigerate until firm.

**MAKES ABOUT 20**

Per ball: 85 calories, 6 g fat, 3 g protein, 6 g carbohydrates, 2 g fiber, 0 mg cholesterol, 2 mg sodium

# PEACH–ALMOND SWIRL

*Sweet, very ripe peaches are the key to the success of this easy dessert. While canned peaches may be substituted for fresh, the difference in flavor will be apparent.*

3/4 cup slivered almonds

1/2 cup water

4 ounces extra-firm silken tofu

5 tablespoons agave syrup or 3/8 teaspoon stevia

1 teaspoon vanilla extract

4–6 peaches, peeled and pitted (see note)

1 teaspoon fresh lemon juice

Grind the almonds to a fine powder in a blender. Add the water and blend until smooth. Add the tofu, 4 tablespoons agave syrup or 1/4 teaspoon stevia, and vanilla; blend until smooth. Transfer to a small bowl, cover, and refrigerate until well chilled.

Slice the peaches; set aside 4 thin slices for garnish and sprinkle them with lemon juice to prevent browning. In a blender or food processor, combine the remaining peaches, remaining lemon juice, and the remaining 1 tablespoon agave syrup or 1/8 teaspoon stevia. Blend until smooth.

Using clear dessert glasses, spoon in alternating spoonfuls of the peach mixture and the almond mixture, leaving swirls of both. Garnish with the reserved peach slices.

## SERVES 4

Per serving: 161 calories, 9 g fat, 6 g protein, 15 g carbohydrates, 4 g fiber, 0 mg cholesterol, 24 mg sodium

Note: To peel peaches, drop the peaches into a pot of boiling water and let stand for 1 minute. Remove with a spoon and plunge into a bowl of ice water. The peels should come off easily.

**Variation:** Substitute yogurt for the tofu.

# ALMOND-ENCRUSTED RED GRAPE TRUFFLES

*The surprising combination of textures and flavors will keep guests coming back for more of these delicious truffle look-alikes. For an impressive presentation, decoratively arrange the grapes on a serving tray garnished with fresh grape leaves. Or serve small clusters of the grapes on individual plates and garnish with a fresh grape leaf.*

> 1 container (8 ounces) tofu cream cheese, at room temperature
> 1 tablespoon soy milk
> 1 cup finely ground toasted almonds
> 2 cups seedless red grapes

In a small bowl, combine the cream cheese and milk. Stir until smooth and creamy, adding a little more milk if necessary to smooth out the cream cheese.

Place the almonds in a shallow bowl or pie plate.

Make sure the grapes are dry. Working with a few at a time, add the grapes to the cream cheese mixture and turn to coat them. Roll the grapes in the almonds to coat, then transfer to a tray or baking sheet.

Refrigerate for at least 1 hour to allow the truffles to firm up before serving.

**SERVES 6**

Per serving: 295 calories, 25 g fat, 8 g protein, 11 g carbohydrates, 3 g fiber, 0 mg cholesterol, 112 mg sodium

**Variation:** Use dairy cream cheese and milk instead of the tofu cream cheese and soy milk.

# WALNUT FUDGE TRUFFLES

*The "dough" will be fairly soft when it first comes out of the food processor, but it should roll up just fine and then firm up nicely in the refrigerator. These tasty bites have the rich flavor of dark chocolate truffles. For a sweeter, slightly firmer truffle, replace the dried plums with dates. Dates are higher in carbs, because of their high natural sugar content.*

½ cup walnut pieces

⅓ cup pitted dried plums (prunes)

½ cup unsweetened cocoa powder

¼ teaspoon stevia, or to taste

4 tablespoons nonhydrogenated, trans-free margarine, at room temperature

Ground toasted walnuts and unsweetened cocoa powder (optional)

Confectioner's sugar

In a food processor, finely grind the walnuts and the dried plums. Add the cocoa, stevia, and margarine; process until well blended. Shape the mixture into 1" balls and place them on a platter or a baking sheet.

Use as is or get a more appealing appearance by rolling the truffles in the ground walnuts or cocoa, or some of each. Cover and refrigerate until firm and keep refrigerated until ready to use. Roll the truffles in confectioner's sugar before serving.

**MAKES 12**

Per truffle: 82 calories, 7 g fat, 1 g protein, 5 g carbohydrates, 2 g fiber, 0 mg cholesterol, 41 mg sodium

**Variation:** Substitute butter for the margarine.

# FRESH STRAWBERRY COULIS

*Lemon juice brings out the natural sweetness of ripe strawberries; however, if you're using berries that aren't very sweet, you may want to add a pinch of stevia, agave syrup, or other natural sweetener.*

**2 cups strawberries**
**½ teaspoon fresh lemon juice**

Place the strawberries and lemon juice in a food processor and blend until smooth. Pour through a fine-mesh strainer into a bowl. Cover and refrigerate until needed.

**SERVES 4**

Per serving: 25 calories, 0 g fat, 0 g protein, 5 g carbohydrates, 2 g fiber, 0 mg cholesterol, 1 mg sodium

# APPENDIX A: CARBOHYDRATE CONTENT OF COMMON FOODS

This chart was derived from information provided in the U.S. Department of Agriculture Nutrient Database and is arranged from highest carbohydrates to lowest. To make it easier to use, I've rounded all figures to the nearest whole number. If you want an even more comprehensive list, go to the Food and Nutrition Information Center (FNIC) Web site at www.nal.usda.gov/fnic/foodcomp/Data; click on "nutrient lists" and then "carbohydrate, sorted by nutrient content."

| Food | Amount | Carbs (grams) | Food | Amount | Carbs (grams) |
|---|---|---|---|---|---|
| Trail mix, tropical | 1 cup | 92 | Tomato paste, canned | 1 cup | 51 |
| Chestnuts, roasted | 1 cup | 76 | Bagel, cinnamon-raisin | 4" bagel | 49 |
| Rhubarb, frozen, cooked, with sugar | 1 cup | 75 | Bagel, plain, enriched | 4" bagel | 48 |
| Potato, french-fried in vegetable oil | 1 large | 67 | Pretzels, hard, plain, salted | 10 pretzels | 48 |
| Graham crackers | 1 cup | 65 | Chickpeas, cooked, boiled | 1 cup | 45 |
| Raisins, seedless | ½ cup | 63 | Rice, brown, long-grain, cooked | 1 cup | 45 |
| Beans, baked, canned, vegetarian | 1 cup | 52 | Prune juice, canned | 1 cup | 45 |
| Applesauce, canned, sweetened | 1 cup | 51 | | | |

| Food | Amount | Carbs (grams) | Food | Amount | Carbs (grams) |
|---|---|---|---|---|---|
| Rice, white, long-grain, cooked | 1 cup | 45 | Spaghetti, whole wheat, cooked | 1 cup | 37 |
| Coconut, dried, sweetened, shredded | 1 cup | 44 | Couscous, cooked | 1 cup | 37 |
| Barley, pearled, cooked | 1 cup | 44 | Cranberry juice cocktail, bottled | 8 fl oz | 36 |
| Beans, pinto, cooked, boiled | 1 cup | 44 | Apricot nectar, canned | 1 cup | 36 |
| Potato, baked | 1 potato | 43 | Sweet potato, cooked, baked in skin | 1 potato | 35 |
| Peas, split, cooked, boiled | 1 cup | 41 | Mangos, raw | 1 mango | 35 |
| Beans, black, cooked, boiled | 1 cup | 41 | Bananas, raw | 1 cup | 35 |
| Beans, kidney, red, cooked | 1 cup | 40 | Lima beans, frozen, baby, cooked | 1 cup | 35 |
| Lentils, cooked, boiled | 1 cup | 40 | Wild rice, cooked | 1 cup | 35 |
| Spaghetti, cooked, enriched | 1 cup | 40 | Pineapple juice, canned, unsweetened | 1 cup | 34 |
| Lima beans, large, cooked, boiled | 1 cup | 39 | Bulgur, cooked | 1 cup | 34 |
| Pineapple, canned, in juice | 1 cup | 39 | Potatoes, baked, flesh, without salt | 1 potato | 34 |
| Carbonated beverage, cola | 12 fl oz | 38 | Black-eyed peas, cooked, boiled, drained | 1 cup | 34 |
| Sweet potato, cooked, boiled | 1 potato | 38 | Buckwheat groats, roasted, cooked | 1 cup | 34 |
| Grape juice, canned or bottled | 1 cup | 38 | Bread, pita, white, enriched | 6½" pita | 33 |
| Beans, great Northern, cooked, boiled | 1 cup | 37 | Corn kernels, yellow, frozen, boiled | 1 cup | 32 |

| Food | Amount | Carbs (grams) | Food | Amount | Carbs (grams) |
|------|--------|---------------|------|--------|---------------|
| Lima beans, frozen, fordhook, cooked | 1 cup | 32 | Pears, raw | 1 pear | 25 |
| Onion rings, breaded and fried | 8–9 rings | 31 | Oat bran, cooked | 1 cup | 25 |
| Potatoes, boiled, cooked without skin, flesh | 1 cup | 31 | Rice beverage, Rice Dream | 1 cup | 25 |
| Dates, domestic, natural, dry | 5 dates | 31 | Figs, dried, uncooked | 2 figs | 25 |
| Parsnips, cooked | 1 cup | 30 | Squash, winter, butternut, frozen, cooked | 1 cup | 24 |
| Papayas, raw | 1 papaya | 30 | Peaches, dried, sulfured, uncooked | 3 halves | 24 |
| Apple juice, unsweetened | 1 cup | 29 | Tomato puree, canned, without salt added | 1 cup | 24 |
| Grapes, red or green seedless, raw | 1 cup | 28 | Peas, green, frozen, cooked | 1 cup | 23 |
| Mangos, raw | 1 cup | 28 | Grapefruit juice | 1 cup | 23 |
| Bananas, raw | 1 banana | 28 | Cranberry sauce, canned, sweetened | 1 slice | 22 |
| Cream of Wheat, regular, cooked | 1 cup | 28 | Carrot juice, canned | 1 cup | 22 |
| Applesauce, canned, unsweetened | 1 cup | 28 | Apricots, dried, sulfured, uncooked | 10 halves | 22 |
| Potatoes, boiled, cooked without skin | 1 potato | 27 | Bread stuffing, bread, dry mix, prepared | ½ cup | 22 |
| Prunes, dried, uncooked | 5 prunes | 26 | Onions, cooked, boiled | 1 cup | 21 |
| Jerusalem artichokes, raw | 1 cup | 26 | Apples, raw, with skin | 1 apple | 21 |
| Oatmeal, regular and quick, cooked | 1 cup | 25 | | | |

| Food | Amount | Carbs (grams) | Food | Amount | Carbs (grams) |
|---|---|---|---|---|---|
| Mushrooms, shiitake, cooked | 1 cup | 21 | Soybeans, cooked, boiled | 1 cup | 17 |
| Bread crumbs, dry, grated, plain | 1 oz | 21 | Beets, cooked, boiled | 1 cup | 17 |
| Pasta sauce, marinara | 1 cup | 21 | Bulgur, cooked | ½ cup | 17 |
| Watermelon, raw | 1 wedge | 21 | Carrots, cooked, boiled | 1 cup | 16 |
| Blueberries, raw | 1 cup | 20 | Apples, raw, without skin | 1 cup | 16 |
| Soybeans, green (edamame), cooked | 1 cup | 20 | Nectarines, raw | 1 nectarine | 16 |
| Pumpkin, canned | 1 cup | 20 | Melons, honeydew, raw | 1 cup | 16 |
| Corn, yellow or white, cooked, boiled | 1 ear | 19 | Bread, pita, white, enriched | 4" pita | 16 |
| Pineapple, raw | 1 cup | 19 | Bread, rye | 1 slice | 15 |
| Peaches, raw | 1 cup | 19 | Oranges, raw | 1 orange | 15 |
| Artichokes, cooked, boiled | 1 cup | 19 | Bread, pumpernickel | 1 slice | 15 |
| Blackberries, raw | 1 cup | 18 | Potato chips, plain, salted | 1 oz | 15 |
| Squash, winter, all varieties, cooked, baked | 1 cup | 18 | Rutabagas, cooked, boiled | 1 cup | 15 |
| Tortilla chips, plain | 1 oz | 18 | Melons, honeydew, raw | ⅛ melon | 15 |
| Tomato sauce, canned | 1 cup | 18 | Raspberries, raw | 1 cup | 14 |
| Water chestnuts, Chinese, canned | 1 cup | 17 | Onions, raw | 1 cup | 14 |
| Honey, strained or extracted | 1 tbsp | 17 | Jams and preserves | 1 tbsp | 14 |
| | | | Papayas, raw | 1 cup | 14 |
| Tomatoes, red, ripe, canned, stewed | 1 cup | 17 | Brussels sprouts, cooked, boiled | 1 cup | 14 |
| | | | Syrup, maple | 1 tbsp | 13 |

| Food | Amount | Carbs (grams) | Food | Amount | Carbs (grams) |
|---|---|---|---|---|---|
| Artichokes, cooked | 1 medium | 13 | Peaches, canned, juice pack | 1 half | 11 |
| Jellies | 1 tbsp | 13 | Kiwifruit, fresh, raw | 1 medium | 11 |
| Cantaloupe, raw | 1 cup | 13 | Peas, edible podded, cooked, boiled | 1 cup | 11 |
| Bread, oatmeal | 1 slice | 13 | | | |
| Pears, Asian, raw | 1 pear | 13 | Cherries, sweet, raw | 10 cherries | 11 |
| Bread, whole wheat | 1 slice | 13 | Carrots, raw | 1 cup | 11 |
| Brussels sprouts, frozen, cooked | 1 cup | 13 | Kohlrabi, cooked, boiled | 1 cup | 11 |
| Beets, canned, drained | 1 cup | 12 | Vegetable juice cocktail, canned | 1 cup | 11 |
| Chocolate syrup | 1 tbsp | 12 | Watermelon, raw | 1 cup | 11 |
| Molasses, blackstrap | 1 tbsp | 12 | Peaches, raw | 1 peach | 11 |
| Tortillas, ready to bake or fry, corn | 1 tortilla | 12 | Graham crackers | 2 squares | 11 |
| Collards, frozen, chopped, cooked, boiled | 1 cup | 12 | Tomatoes, red, ripe, canned, whole | 1 cup | 10 |
| Bread, mixed grain | 1 slice | 12 | Tomato juice, canned | 1 cup | 10 |
| Carrots, frozen, cooked, boiled | 1 cup | 12 | Spinach, frozen, chopped or leaf, cooked | 1 cup | 10 |
| Pumpkin, cooked, boiled | 1 cup | 12 | | | |
| Bread, wheat (includes wheatberry) | 1 slice | 12 | Sauerkraut, canned, solids and liquids | 1 cup | 10 |
| Strawberries, raw | 1 cup | 12 | Bread, Italian | 1 slice | 10 |
| Okra, cooked, boiled | 1 cup | 12 | Grapefruit, raw, white | ½ grapefruit | 10 |

| Food | Amount | Carbs (grams) | Food | Amount | Carbs (grams) |
|---|---|---|---|---|---|
| Beans, snap, cooked, boiled | 1 cup | 10 | Beans, snap, yellow, frozen, cooked, boiled | 1 cup | 9 |
| Broccoli, frozen, chopped, cooked, boiled | 1 cup | 10 | Plums, raw | 1 plum | 9 |
| Pears, canned, juice pack | 1 half | 10 | Crackers, saltines | 4 crackers | 9 |
| Baking chocolate, unsweetened, liquid | 1 oz | 10 | Cashew nuts, oil roasted | 1 oz (18 nuts) | 9 |
| Peppers, sweet, red or green, raw | 1 cup | 10 | Tomatoes, red, ripe, raw | 1 cup | 8 |
| Onions, cooked, boiled | 1 medium | 10 | Cucumber, with peel, raw | 1 large | 8 |
| Onions, raw | 1 whole | 9 | Taco shells, baked | 1 medium | 8 |
| Grapefruit, raw, pink and red | ½ grapefruit | 9 | Turnip greens, frozen, cooked, boiled | 1 cup | 8 |
| Collards, cooked, boiled | 1 cup | 9 | Baking chocolate, unsweetened, squares | 1 square | 8 |
| Cashew nuts, dry roasted | 1 oz | 9 | Mushrooms, cooked, boiled | 1 cup | 8 |
| Peppers, sweet, red or green, cooked | 1 cup | 9 | Popcorn, cakes | 1 cake | 8 |
| Orange juice, raw from | 1 orange | 9 | Sugars, powdered | 1 tbsp | 8 |
| Grapes, red or green, raw | 10 grapes | 9 | Leeks, cooked, boiled | 1 cup | 8 |
| Asparagus, frozen, cooked, boiled | 1 cup | 9 | Broccoli, cooked, boiled | 1 cup | 8 |
| Beans, snap, green, frozen, cooked, boiled | 1 cup | 9 | Beet greens, cooked, boiled | 1 cup | 8 |
| | | | Squash, summer, fall varieties, cooked | 1 cup | 8 |

| Food | Amount | Carbs (grams) | Food | Amount | Carbs (grams) |
|---|---|---|---|---|---|
| Mushrooms, canned | 1 cup | 8 | Cucumber, peeled, raw | 1 large | 7 |
| Sunflower seed kernels, dry roasted | ¼ cup | 8 | Coconut meat, raw | 1 piece | 7 |
| Peppers, sweet, red or green, raw | 1 pepper | 8 | Sunflower seed kernels, dry roasted | 1 oz | 7 |
| Turnips, cooked, boiled | 1 cup | 8 | Kale, frozen, cooked, boiled | 1 cup | 7 |
| Pistachio nuts, dry roasted | 1 oz (47 nuts) | 8 | Cauliflower, frozen, cooked, boiled | 1 cup | 7 |
| Morningstar Farms Better'n Burger, frozen | 1 patty | 8 | Spinach, cooked, boiled | 1 cup | 7 |
| Pineapple, canned, juice pack | 1 slice | 7 | Dandelion greens, cooked, boiled | 1 cup | 7 |
| Scallions or spring onions, raw | 1 cup | 7 | Cabbage, cooked, boiled | 1 cup | 7 |
| Rice cakes, brown rice, plain | 1 cake | 7 | Morningstar Farms "Burger" Crumbles | 1 cup | 7 |
| Kale, cooked, boiled | 1 cup | 7 | Eggplant, cooked, boiled | 1 cup | 7 |
| Carrots, raw | 1 carrot | 7 | Popcorn, oil popped | 1 cup | 6 |
| Spinach, canned, drained | 1 cup | 7 | Turnip greens, cooked, boiled | 1 cup | 6 |
| Apple butter | 1 tbsp | 7 | Popcorn, air popped | 1 cup | 6 |
| Mixed nuts, dry roasted, with peanuts | 1 oz | 7 | Mung beans, sprouted, raw | 1 cup | 6 |
| Carambola (star fruit), raw | 1 fruit | 7 | Peanuts, dry roasted | 1 oz (approx 28) | 6 |
| Hoisin sauce, ready to serve | 1 tbsp | 7 | Celery, cooked, boiled | 1 cup | 6 |

| Food | Amount | Carbs (grams) | Food | Amount | Carbs (grams) |
|---|---|---|---|---|---|
| Melons, cantaloupe, raw | ⅛ melon | 6 | Sugars, granulated | 1 tsp | 4 |
| Tomatoes, red, ripe, raw | 1 tomato | 6 | Onions, dehydrated flakes | 1 tbsp | 4 |
| Almonds | 1 oz (24 nuts) | 6 | Ketchup | 1 tbsp | 4 |
| Lemons, raw, without peel | 1 lemon | 5 | Lemon juice, raw juice of | 1 lemon | 4 |
| Peanuts, oil roasted | 1 oz | 5 | Pine nuts, pignolia, dried | 1 oz | 4 |
| Pickle relish, sweet | 1 tbsp | 5 | Artichoke hearts (frozen) | 3 oz | 4 |
| Cauliflower, raw | 1 cup | 5 | | | |
| Mung beans, sprouted, cooked | 1 cup | 5 | Vegetarian sausage (Gimme Lean) | 2 oz | 4 |
| Cauliflower, cooked, boiled | 1 cup | 5 | Pecans | 1 oz (20 halves) | 4 |
| Lightlife Smart Deli "Ham Slices" | 4 slices | 5 | Apricots, raw | 1 apricot | 4 |
| Beets, cooked, boiled | 1 beet | 5 | Walnuts, English | 1 oz (14 halves) | 4 |
| Squash, summer, all varieties, raw | 1 cup | 5 | Pumpkin seed kernels, roasted | 1 oz (142 seeds) | 4 |
| Hazelnuts or filberts | 1 oz | 5 | Cabbage, raw | 1 cup | 4 |
| Broccoli, raw | 1 cup | 5 | Lettuce, butterhead, raw | 1 head | 4 |
| Soy milk, fluid | 1 cup | 4 | Macadamia nuts, dry roasted | 1 oz (10–12 nuts) | 4 |
| Celery, raw | 1 cup | 4 | | | |
| Cabbage, red, raw | 1 cup | 4 | Brazil nuts, dried, unblanched | 1 oz (6–8 nuts) | 4 |
| Cabbage, Savoy, raw | 1 cup | 4 | Wheat germ, toasted, plain | 1 tbsp | 4 |
| Peppers, hot chile, red or green, raw | 1 pepper | 4 | | | |
| Bamboo shoots, canned | 1 cup | 4 | Peanut butter, chunk style, with salt | 1 tbsp | 3 |

| Food | Amount | Carbs (grams) | Food | Amount | Carbs (grams) |
|---|---|---|---|---|---|
| Lime juice, raw juice of | 1 lime | 3 | Cauliflower, cooked, boiled | 3 florets | 2 |
| Tahini paste (sesame butter) | 1 tbsp | 3 | Tofu, soft | ¼ block | 2 |
| Sugars, brown | 1 tsp | 3 | Barbecue sauce | 1 tbsp | 2 |
| Peanut butter, smooth style | 1 tbsp | 3 | Hummus, commercial | 1 tbsp | 2 |
| Miso paste | 1 tbsp | 3 | Tomatillos, raw | 1 medium | 2 |
| Cucumber, peeled, raw | 1 cup | 3 | Lettuce, looseleaf, raw | 1 cup | 2 |
| Mustard greens, cooked, boiled | 1 cup | 3 | Avocados, raw, California | 1 oz | 2 |
| Candies, hard | 1 small piece | 3 | Broccoli, cooked, boiled | 1 spear | 2 |
| Cocoa, dry powder, unsweetened | 1 tbsp | 3 | Asparagus, canned, drained | 4 spears | 2 |
| Teriyaki sauce | 1 tbsp | 3 | Beets, canned | 1 beet | 2 |
| Cucumber, with peel, raw | 1 cup | 3 | Shallots, raw | 1 tbsp | 2 |
| Cabbage, Chinese, cooked, boiled | 1 cup | 3 | Endive, raw | 1 cup | 2 |
| Mushrooms, raw | 1 cup | 3 | Hearts of palm, canned | 1 piece | 2 |
| Mushrooms, shiitake, dried | 1 mushroom | 3 | Celery, raw | 1 stalk | 1 |
| Pickles, cucumber, dill | 1 pickle | 3 | Olives, ripe, canned (small–extra large) | 5 large | 1 |
| Asparagus, cooked, boiled | 4 spears | 3 | Soy sauce (shoyu) | 1 tbsp | 1 |
| Avocados, raw, Florida | 1 oz | 3 | Lettuce, cos or romaine, raw | 1 cup | 1 |
| Tofu, firm | ¼ block | 2 | Alfalfa seeds, sprouted, raw | 1 cup | 1 |
| | | | Peppers, jalapeño, canned | ¼ cup | 1 |

| Food | Amount | Carbs (grams) | Food | Amount | Carbs (grams) |
|---|---|---|---|---|---|
| Pine nuts, pignolia, dried | 1 tbsp | 1 | Strawberries, raw | 1 strawberry | 1 |
| Onions, raw | 1 slice | 1 | Carrots, baby, raw | 1 medium | 1 |
| Lettuce, iceberg, raw | 1 cup | 1 | Cherry tomato, red, ripe, raw | 1 average | 1 |
| Tomatoes, sun-dried | 1 piece | 1 | Sesame seed kernels, dried | 1 tbsp | 1 |
| Scallions or spring onion, raw | 1 whole | 1 | Tomatoes, sun-dried, packed in oil, drained | 1 piece | 1 |
| Spinach, raw | 1 cup | 1 | Cauliflower, raw | 1 floret | 1 |
| Lime juice, canned or bottled | 1 tbsp | 1 | Peppers, sweet, green, raw | 1 ring | 1 |
| Salsa, ready-to-serve | 1 tbsp | 1 | Broccoli, flower clusters, raw | 1 floret | 1 |
| Garlic, raw | 1 clove | 1 | Horseradish, prepared | 1 tsp | 1 |
| Lemon juice, canned or bottled | 1 tbsp | 1 | Arugula, raw | ½ cup | 0 |
| Seaweed, kelp, raw | 2 tbsp | 1 | Radishes, raw | 1 radish | 0 |
| Tomatoes, red, ripe, raw | 1 slice | 1 | Oil, olive, canola, or sesame | 1 tbsp | 0 |

# APPENDIX B: GLYCEMIC INDEX CHART

Here are the glycemic index (GI) values of some common foods. The lower the value, the better. There are two standards used for the glycemic index: white bread and glucose. This index uses glucose as the benchmark of 100. For more information on the glycemic index and glycemic loads or to look up the glycemic index of particular foods as provided by the International Table of Glycemic Index, visit the Web site www.glycemicindex.com.

GI Values of Common Foods

High GI = 70 or greater

Medium GI = 55 to 69

Low GI = 54 or below

Ratings listed from high to low within each category.

| Vegetables | | Corn | 55 |
|---|---|---|---|
| Parsnips | 95 | Sweet potato | 54 |
| Potato (baked) | 85 | Green peas | 48 |
| Potato (mashed) | 80 | Artichoke | <15 |
| Potato (french fries) | 75 | Asparagus | <15 |
| Pumpkin | 75 | Bell peppers | <15 |
| Carrots | 71 | Broccoli | <15 |
| Rutabaga | 71 | Cabbage | <15 |
| Beets | 69 | Cauliflower | <15 |
| Potato (new) | 62 | Celery | <15 |

| | | | |
|---|---|---|---|
| Chiles | <15 | Papaya | 58 |
| Cucumber | <15 | Banana | 55 |
| Eggplant | <15 | Mango | 55 |
| Green beans | <15 | Kiwi | 52 |
| Greens (collards, kale, etc.) | <15 | Grapes | 46 |
| Lettuce (all varieties) | <15 | Orange | 44 |
| Mushrooms | <15 | Apple | 36 |
| Onions | <15 | Pear | 36 |
| Spinach | <15 | Strawberries | 32 |
| Summer squash | <15 | Prunes | 29 |
| Tomatoes | <15 | Peach | 28 |
| Zucchini | <15 | Grapefruit | 25 |
| | | Plum | 25 |
| **Beans and Legumes** | | Cherries | 22 |
| Pinto beans | 39 | | |
| Navy beans | 38 | **Grains** | |
| Chickpeas | 33 | Short-grain white rice | 72 |
| Lima beans | 32 | Arborio rice | 69 |
| Cannellini beans | 31 | Basmati rice | 58 |
| White beans | 31 | Wild rice | 57 |
| Black beans | 30 | Long-grain white rice | 56 |
| Lentils | 30 | Brown rice | 55 |
| Red kidney beans | 27 | Bulgur | 48 |
| Soybeans | 18 | | |
| | | **Breakfast Cereal** | |
| **Fruit** | | Puffed rice | 95 |
| Dates | 103 | Cornflakes | 84 |
| Watermelon | 75 | Shredded wheat | 70 |
| Pineapple | 66 | All-Bran | 55 |
| Cantaloupe | 65 | Special K | 54 |
| Raisins | 64 | Oatmeal (not instant) | 40 |

## Grain Products

| | |
|---|---|
| Baguette | 95 |
| White bread | 95 |
| Rice pasta | 92 |
| Doughnut | 76 |
| Rye bread | 76 |
| Waffles | 76 |
| Kaiser roll | 73 |
| Bagel | 72 |
| Corn tortilla | 72 |
| Taco shells | 68 |
| Croissant | 67 |
| Refined pasta | 65 |
| Bran muffin | 60 |
| Pita bread | 57 |
| Stone-ground whole wheat bread | 53 |
| Whole grain bread | 40–50 |
| Whole grain pasta | 5 |

## Beverages

| | |
|---|---|
| Soft drink | 68 |
| Cranberry juice cocktail | 52 |
| Orange juice | 52 |
| Grapefruit juice | 48 |
| Carrot juice | 45 |
| Apple juice | 41 |
| Tomato juice | 37 |
| Soy milk | 30 |

## Sweeteners

| | |
|---|---|
| Maltose | 105 |
| Glucose | 100 |
| Sucrose (table sugar) | 65 |
| Honey | 58 |
| Fructose | 23 |
| Agave syrup | 11 |

## Snacks and Treats

| | |
|---|---|
| Jelly beans | 80 |
| Pretzels | 80 |
| Corn chips | 73 |
| Life Savers | 70 |
| Popcorn | 55 |
| Potato chips | 55 |
| Strawberry jam | 51 |
| Chocolate bar | 49 |
| Cashews | 22 |
| Dark chocolate (70% cocoa) | 22 |
| Walnuts | 15 |
| Peanuts | 14 |

## Cookies and Crackers

| | |
|---|---|
| Rice crackers | 91 |
| Rice cakes | 82 |
| Water crackers | 78 |
| Vanilla wafers | 77 |
| Graham crackers | 74 |
| Soda crackers (saltines, etc.) | 74 |
| Melba toast | 70 |
| Stoned wheat thins | 67 |
| Shortbread cookies | 64 |
| Oatmeal cookies | 55 |

# GLYCEMIC LOAD CHART

Low GL = 10 or less
Medium GL = 11 to 19
High GL = 20 or more

**Examples of Low-Glycemic-Load Foods
(10 or Less)**
Black-eyed peas
Carrots
Chickpeas
Kidney beans
Lima beans
Pinto beans

Split peas
White beans
Whole grains

**Examples of High-Glycemic-Load Foods
(20 or More)**
Cookies
Crackers
White bread
White pasta
White potatoes
White rice

# RECIPE INDEX

## Z

Zucchini

Carrot and Zucchini "Linguine" with
Edamame, Black Olives, and Arugula
Pesto, 140

Chili con Veggies, 61

Eggplant Stuffed with Zucchini, Cauliflower,
and Sun-Dried Tomatoes, 126

Jamaican Roasted Vegetables, 131

Many-Vegetable Bulgur Pilaf, 156

Old-Fashioned Vegetable Soup, 40

Pecan-Studded Apple-Zucchini Cake, 200–201

Raid-the-Garden Ratatouille, 115

Simmered Zucchini with Onion and Tomatoes,
96

Sinless Shepherd's Pie, 142–43

Spice-Rubbed Vegetable Kebabs, 144–45

Summer Squash "Paglia e Fieno" with Creamy
Cashew Sauce, 153

Summer Vegetable Bisque, 47

Three-Bean Minestrone Soup, 42

Very Veggie Burgers with "Basic Black" Bean
Sauce, 146

Victory Garden Stew, 62

White Bean and Chard-Stuffed Zucchini with
Red Pepper Coulis, 154–55

Zucchini Fettuccine Puttanesca, 152

# GENERAL INDEX

# CONVERSION CHART

These equivalents have been slightly rounded to make measuring easier.

VOLUME MEASUREMENTS

| U.S. | Imperial | Metric |
|---|---|---|
| ¼ tsp | – | 1 ml |
| ½ tsp | – | 2 ml |
| 1 tsp | – | 5 ml |
| 1 Tbsp | – | 15 ml |
| 2 Tbsp (1 oz) | 1 fl oz | 30 ml |
| ¼ cup (2 oz) | 2 fl oz | 60 ml |
| ⅓ cup (3 oz) | 3 fl oz | 80 ml |
| ½ cup (4 oz) | 4 fl oz | 120 ml |
| ⅔ cup (5 oz) | 5 fl oz | 160 ml |
| ¾ cup (6 oz) | 6 fl oz | 180 ml |
| 1 cup (8 oz) | 8 fl oz | 240 ml |

WEIGHT MEASUREMENTS

| U.S. | Metric |
|---|---|
| 1 oz | 30 g |
| 2 oz | 60 g |
| 4 oz (¼ lb) | 115 g |
| 5 oz (⅓ lb) | 145 g |
| 6 oz | 170 g |
| 7 oz | 200 g |
| 8 oz (½ lb) | 230 g |
| 10 oz | 285 g |
| 12 oz (¾ lb) | 340 g |
| 14 oz | 400 g |
| 16 oz (1 lb) | 455 g |
| 2.2 lb | 1 kg |

LENGTH MEASUREMENTS

| U.S. | Metric |
|---|---|
| ¼" | 0.6 cm |
| ½" | 1.25 cm |
| 1" | 2.5 cm |
| 2" | 5 cm |
| 4" | 11 cm |
| 6" | 15 cm |
| 8" | 20 cm |
| 10" | 25 cm |
| 12" (1') | 30 cm |

PAN SIZES

| U.S. | Metric |
|---|---|
| 8" cake pan | 20 × 4 cm sandwich or cake tin |
| 9" cake pan | 23 × 3.5 cm sandwich or cake tin |
| 11" × 7" baking pan | 28 × 18 cm baking tin |
| 13" × 9" baking pan | 32.5 × 23 cm baking tin |
| 15" × 10" baking pan | 38 × 25.5 cm baking tin (Swiss roll tin) |
| 1½ qt baking dish | 1.5 liter baking dish |
| 2 qt baking dish | 2 liter baking dish |
| 2 qt rectangular baking dish | 30 × 19 cm baking dish |
| 9" pie plate | 22 × 4 or 23 × 4 cm pie plate |
| 7" or 8" springform pan | 18 or 20 cm springform or loose-bottom cake tin |
| 9" × 5" loaf pan | 23 × 13 cm or 2 lb narrow loaf tin or pâté tin |

TEMPERATURES

| Fahrenheit | Centigrade | Gas |
|---|---|---|
| 140° | 60° | – |
| 160° | 70° | – |
| 180° | 80° | – |
| 225° | 105° | ¼ |
| 250° | 120° | ½ |
| 275° | 135° | 1 |
| 300° | 150° | 2 |
| 325° | 160° | 3 |
| 350° | 180° | 4 |
| 375° | 190° | 5 |
| 400° | 200° | 6 |
| 425° | 220° | 7 |
| 450° | 230° | 8 |
| 475° | 245° | 9 |
| 500° | 260° | – |